The Zodiac Killer. This is been a lot of work over the years. It is a thankless job, but that is not why people like myself do this. We do it because we love it. Seeing mysterious symbols and puzzles, wondering what kind of secrets they hold. It is about the closest thing to something that is actually magical we may find in this world. This book is for the people of the future. While it will probably be ignored in my time, the time will come when it will be useful. That is if Zodiac isn't caught sometime in the near future using DNA and genealogy web sites. The way the Golden State Killer and the NorCal rapist have been recently captured. If he is still out there (and I believe there is a good chance that he still is) I guarantee that he is worried. If his identity isn't discovered soon, then I fear it never conclusively will be. It will be relegated to legend just the way Jack the Ripper has been. In a way, that might be best. Somewhere deep down inside of this monster, he wants the credit for fooling everyone for all of these years. He wants the credit and recognition for his so-called "brilliant crimes". That is how he views it in his own head anyway. The truth is, he was just a cowardly little man desperate for attention that he could not attain. I say that we don't let him have it. One of the things that probably eats away at him is the fact that so many others have gotten the credit for his crimes. Credit, it's funny we use that word when talking about such sick and sadistic acts. We should be using the word blame. Hollywood and popular culture have elevated the Zodiac killer from the scum of the earth to immortal fame. Let's not forget the people he hurt and the lives he took away from so many innocent young people who had their whole lives ahead of them. And for what? For what? It was pointless. The pain their families felt was very real, and sometimes it can be easy to forget that these were real people who actually existed. Don't forget David Faraday, Betty Jensen, Darlene Ferrin, and Paul Stine. The unknown number of other people whose lives he has taken away and the families whose lives he destroyed deserve justice. They deserve closure. Don't forget that the surviving victims and the families of the victims are all still out there. Everyone should be mindful of that. If they can't get justice, then they at least deserve peace. If he is ever caught, then I hope is he seen for what he really was and not what culture has built him up to be. He sent some codes that were never solved. So, what. That doesn't make him special. They did, however, keep the case from being forgotten, and in the end, the very thing he was so proud of may just be his undoing. Wouldn't that be poetic justice?

CONTENTS

CHAPTER 1 – IN THE BEGINNING

Once upon a time, in a land far, far away, there was once a man, okay, maybe it wasn't that far away. The time was 1969 and the land was a mystical and magical place called San Francisco. This man called himself…., Zodiac. No one knew who this man really was, where he came from, or what happened to him. All we know is what he did, what he wanted us to know, and that out of all the kinds of crazy this man could be, he was "bat shit". The worst kind of crazy there is. Though he told us only what he wanted us to know, he may have revealed things he never intended to reveal in the many letters and codes he created and sent to the police and newspapers. They say that only one of his codes was ever solved. I am about to prove that wrong by showing you another code that no one even knew he created. What is it, you may ask? You have just seen it on the cover of this book. While the mainstream chooses to ignore it, anyone with eyes can see.

On the night of December 20th, 1968, a Friday night. Seventeen-year-old David Faraday had been getting ready for his first real date. A big night for anyone, no doubt. A night that he would have remembered for the rest of his life.

David had been allowed to borrow his father's Rambler Station Wagon, to go pick up his date, 16-year-old Betty Lou Jensen. Both were high school students who were on the cusp of adulthood. Their entire lives were ahead of them.

I am sure Betty Lou was very excited as she got ready for what would be her first date also. You can imagine what both of the teenagers were feeling and thinking. We have all been there, feeling the temporary high of the drug call love.

The young couple at least had this one night together. Sometime before the two were supposed to return home, they decided to do what most in their situation would have done. They went to find a private place to be alone. In a speck of secluded dirt turn off on Lake Herman Road. About five miles east of a town called Vallejo.

No one really knows the exact events that took place, and anyone who says otherwise is either a liar or a suspect. We know it went something like this from the investigation that was conducted by the police.

As the two were parked in their car, an unknown man happened upon them. No one knows if he had been stalking them or if it was a crime of opportunity. What led their paths to cross has been a popular question. We know the man pulled his car up in front of them to block their escape and ordered them out their car either by gunpoint or by some other form of persuasion.

The man then ordered David Faraday to get down on his knees by gunpoint while Betty Lou watched in horror. As in most of the other known crimes he committed, he liked to make the female watch what was about to happen to her as he brutalized the male. A form of psychological torture.

As Betty watched, helpless to do anything, the man put his 22-caliber pistol to David's head, just behind the left ear, and pulled the trigger. He shot him in true execution fashion. I can't help but wonder where he learned this from. Movies, books, or somewhere else? Remember, this was the 1960's.

When Betty heard the gunshot and saw David's body fall lifeless to the ground, she did what any sensible person in that terrifying situation would have done. The instinct of fight or flight overcame her, and she turned to run away. I believe this was the reaction the man had wanted all along. He enjoyed the terror he imposed onto others. Like a wild animal stalking its prey, the predator enjoyed the chase. He eluded to this in one of his codes when he referenced a book, 'The Most Dangerous Game'. He didn't see Betty as a person, he saw her as the epitome of everything he hated and he would make her pay.

As Betty made her futile attempt to run away, she had probably hoped the darkness would help hide her from some of the bullets that she knew were meant for her. As the adrenaline coursed through her system, with her heart pounding, time probably seemed to slow down for her. She knew that her death was imminent and God only knows what other horrors she imagined could be in store for her. As she attempted to save her own life, Betty heard five other shots ring out into the still night. One at a time, each of the five other bullets that were loaded into the killer's 22 caliber J.C. Higgins model pistol found their way into the right side of Betty's back. No one ever imagines this can happen to them. It was like a nightmare she couldn't wake from. In the very end, she fell to the ground twenty-eight feet from the back of David's father's Rambler Station Wagon. Other than the man who had robbed her of her young life, she was completely alone. No one to comfort her, no one to help her. There, she took her last breath as the dark overcame her. She was 16.

The killer would later claim he had taped a small flashlight to the barrel of his gun to aid him in the dark. Any small flashlight is referred to as a penlight, though in his letter he called it a "pencil light". For almost half a year this crime would remain a mystery without a clue to who had committed it, or why. Later, someone would come forward.

July 4th, 1969, another Friday night. 19-year-old Michael Mageau had been picked up by twenty-two-year-old Darlene Ferrin. The two would drive around the Vallejo, California area enjoying the 4th of July on one of the most famous years in history. Over the years, the story has changed from time to time. That is to be expected as time passes, but unlike the first attack on Lake Herman Road, this one would have a survivor.

Darlene was a married woman, and she was out with a single man. That doesn't mean anything was going on. It also doesn't mean they wouldn't try to spark some sort of romantic connection.

Just as in the first attack, the two made their way to a secluded parking lot across the street from the Blue Rock Springs golf course east of Vallejo. They were in the parking lot of a local park. Just five miles north of the site where the Faraday/Jensen murders occurred, and just a stone's throw from the mouth of Lake Herman Road.

It is said that other people were in the area when this attack occurred, but not in the parking lot. As the two were sitting in Darlene's Chevy Corvair conversating, Michael later stated that a vehicle had pulled in behind them with the lights on bright. He described it as something a police officer would have done because he rolled down his window expecting to have to talk to one. Some say the window was already down. Others have also made connections to the Zodiac and the police, but you have to find that on your own and decide for yourself.

As Michael rolled down the passenger door window, someone exited the car behind the two and proceeded to walk to his door instead of the driver's as one might expect a police officer to do. In his first letter, Zodiac stated that the window was already rolled down, which it being the middle of summer, it probably was. As he approached the car, it is said he had turned on a bright light and shined it in their eyes to blind them, as a police officer might do.

Before Michael could get any words out, shots rang out into the car. Being 4th of July night, they may have blended right in with the fireworks or been mistaken for them. Five shots from a nine-millimeter semi-automatic were fired at random into the vehicle, aiming for no particular place on their bodies.

Michael, acting almost in reflex, flung himself into the back seat of the car in an attempt to shield himself from the bullets. The attacker must have thought he had done the job when he turned to walk away until he heard a sound coming from inside of the car. He then turned around and fired four more shots into the car. Michael said that he never said a word.

A Little later that night, a phone would ring at the local police station. A lady by the name of Nancy Slover would answer the call only to hear someone in a monotone voice say, "**I want to report a double murder. If you go one mile east on the Columbus Parkway, to the public park, you will find the kids in the brown car. They were shot with a nine-millimeter luger. I also killed those kids last year. Goodbye.**"

The kids he referred to killing that last year were David and Betty. An interesting thing that is never hardly mentioned. In the 2009 documentary 'This is the Zodiac Speaking', Nancy Slover stated in an interview that this was not the only call she had received that night reporting the attack. She stated that she had also gotten a call from a woman who had reported the very same attack. This woman was never identified and could have held valuable information that could have cracked the whole case wide open. It was reported that this was a secluded area with no one around at the time, but this statement from Nancy says otherwise. We may never know who the woman was, or what she witnessed.

When police got on the scene, they found the two inside of the car near the point of death. Darlene was pronounced dead later that night at the hospital while Michael would survive the attack and go on to have a long life. Both will live forever in history.

Michael's story would change from time to time over the

years, but in fairness, that is to be expected. He once even identified a man by the name of Arthur Leigh Allen as the person who had attacked them that night in a picture line-up. Arthur, a long-suspected Zodiac possibility, would have his name cleared of the crimes only after his death. DNA evidence would prove he was not the Zodiac. Don't feel too bad for old Arthur, he wasn't that great of a guy. There is a reason he was a suspect.

A few months later in late September 27th, 1969, there was yet another attack. This time on a Saturday, during the day. Twenty-year-old Bryan Hartnell had picked up and old girlfriend, twenty-two-year-old Cecilia Shepard, to catch up on old times. Bryan, a college student who became a prominent attorney later in life, would survive this attack just as Michael did.

The two young college students decided to go to a secluded spot by a place called Lake Berryessa that was located north of Vallejo, California. Less than a mile from the park ranger headquarters. You have to ask yourself, was this by design or coincidence?

According to Richard Grinell's work, several people had reported a strange individual watching them in the time leading up to the attack less than one mile away from what would become the crime scene.

Three women had reported a suspicious individual observing them from a hillside near where they had stated they parked their vehicle. This location was two miles north of an A & W Root Beer stand on Knoxville Road, near where the attack was about to take place.

This was followed by a second sighting of a suspicious individual by a Dr. Rayfield and his son just over 2 hours later. They had described a **"white male adult subject walking in the area, about 5'10", with a heavy build, who was wearing dark trousers, a dark shirt with red on it, and long sleeves"**. According to Richard (who is very thorough), this sighting probably happened after the attack at a **"location approximately 8/10ths of a mile from the scene of the victim's vehicle"**. Two different reports in the same area, alongside a place called 'Smittle Creek Trailhead', that occurred before and after the attack.

It is believed this strange man who had been watching the three young ladies was likely spotting them out like a hunter would spot a dear before deciding to move and running across Bryan and Cecilia lying on a secluded peninsula that jutted out into the lake. This goes back to the reference of the book **'The Most Dangerous Game'**.

As the two were lying on the peninsula at Lake Berryessa idly chatting, Cecilia noticed a man watching them from behind a tree, just like the man the three women had reported earlier. When she alarmed Bryan that they were being surveilled by someone, Bryan initially shrugged it off and paid no attention. Right up to the point that Cecilia informed him that the man who had been watching them was wearing a mask, pointing a gun, and walking toward them.

Out of all of the attacks that occurred, this is one of the most interesting. This is because some claim this was a break in the pattern of the attacks. Was it? There had been only two known attacks and no real proof to link Zodiac to the first attack on Lake Herman road other than an unknown man confessing to it.

With only two attacks, there is not enough information to establish a solid pattern, which means you could be looking at the wrong pattern. Everyone does follow some kind of pattern, whether they know it or not, but to establish a pattern, you have to have more than two sources of information to base it on.

But let's say we do have a pattern. Why was this a break in the pattern? What made this attack different from the first two? **1**. It took place during the day. **2**. He was wearing a mask. **3**. The most important, he used a knife.

After the man approached the two, he pulled out some lengths of precut rope and ordered Cecelia to tie up Bryan while holding her at gunpoint.

While this was happening, Bryan was trying to have a conversation with the man. This may seem crazy, but it is the best thing you could possibly do in a situation like that. This is an attempt to humanize yourself to your attacker while also maybe gleaning some information from him about himself. Bryan had initially thought to attempt an attack the man and try to wrestle away the gun, but Cecelia had read on his face what he was thinking and signaled to him by shaking her head not to try. One can only wonder how things may have played out differently if he had followed his instincts. If he had known what was about to take place, he would have realized he had nothing to lose. Hindsight is 20/20 and at the time they thought it might just be a simple robbery.

After Cecilia had tied Bryan's hands behind his back, he was ordered to lye down as the man then tied Cecilia's hands behind her back, after which he then retied Bryan's restraints.

In the ensuing conversation, the man told them that he had escaped from prison. After that point, different stories about this would be told over the following years and it can be hard to tell what is fact and what is honest mistake or fiction. There is some talk that he mentioned Deer Lodge prison in Montana. In a letter that would come years later, he refers to a movie called **'The Badlands'**. This too is a reference to a place in Montana.

According to Bryan, the man was wearing a hooded bib over his head. The hood was square at the top with four sharp corners, like a paper bag. The hood was black in appearance with a crossed white circle on the bib of the hood over the chest. Bryan stated, "It looked quality made".

Bryan and Cecilia thought that if they cooperated they would go about their lives and have an interesting story to tell. Just when they thought the encounter was about to end, Cecilia watched in horror as the man suddenly pulled out his knife and began to violently stab Bryan. Just as in the other attacks, the attacker began with the male subject first before moving on the female. I believe this was to punish the female even more by making her watch what was about to happen to her. He got off on terrorizing the female.

Bryan was stabbed in the back six times before the man moved on to Cecilia. Bryan pretended to be dead as he heard the screams from Cecilia when the knife entered her body. In some sort of an excited frenzy, the man went wild on Cecilia, stabbing her over and over and over, in the front and back. She died three days later on September 29th.

After the killer left the scene, Bryan, bleeding and in great pain, forced himself to crawl from the spot on the peninsula to the roadway, 510 yards away. He was thinking more about Cecilia than he was for himself.

There are reports that people who were fishing out on the lake may have seen the two on the peninsula and a house that was visible across the water may have played some sort of a role. No one really knows but there are lots of reports and stories out there that can be studied if you look for them.

The killer then drove to a nearby payphone and reported the attack to the police. The normal operator at the police station was on break, as another officer had relieved him. When the phone rang, just like Nancy Slover had, the officer took the call and heard the words, "**I want to report a murder, no, a double murder. They are two miles north of park headquarters. They were in a white Volkswagon Karman Ghia. I'm the one who did it.**"

He then put the phone down, letting it just hang

without ending the call. The officer reported hearing people in the background. A local reporter who had been listening to a police scanner heard what was going on. He then drove around the area shouting out, "Can you hear me?", until they found the phone the call had been made from.

Contrary to popular belief, and according to reports, evidence was collected from this phone. They said, "The prints were so fresh that we had to artificially dry them out to take them."

Another interesting fact pointed out by Richard Grinell in his work, Zodiac said the attack occurred two miles from park headquarters when in reality it was less than a mile. The payphone Zodiac made the call from was two miles from park headquarters, this is an interesting mistake by the killer and not his only mistake. It proves he could make mistakes, whether they were honest or otherwise. In one of his first letters, he made a mistake about the clothing one of his victims had been wearing. He stated that she had been wearing patterned slacks when in fact she has been wearing a patterned dress. The girl he was referring to was Darlene Ferrin. Some have grasped onto this as proof that all of this was a hoax, possibly even perpetrated by a police officer, but remember that is was dark and the entire encounter only lasted a few seconds. It could have just been a simple mistake and who knows if he had been drunk or high. Even people who think it was all a hoax think that someone involved with the police may have had something to do with it. He was obsessed with playing with the police. That is interesting, but who knows. Maybe one day we may find out.

Bryan would live to tell his story, never being able to escape it, and while Cecilia did not survive, both individuals will live forever in history. Entertwined forever in the legend of one of the most famous serial murderers second only to Jack the Ripper.

October 11th, 1969. Twenty-nine-year-old taxi driver Paul Lee Stine had just begun his shift. He had just picked up his first fair of the night. After entering the taxi, the passenger instructed Paul to take him to the corner of Washington and Maple in the Presidio Heights area of San Francisco, according to the taxi log kept by Paul.

Like the first attack, no one really knows what happened inside of that cab as the two drove through the city, but we know after reaching their destination, the passenger instructed Paul to take him one block further to the corner of Washington and Cherry. These two words together remind one of the famous stories about George Washington chopping down his father's cherry tree. Every American schoolchild has heard this story.

As the car came to stop at the corner of Washington and Cherry, two children playing in the home across the street witnessed the events that took place from an upstairs window.

The children told police that they had seen a man get out of the cab and walk over to the driver's side window of the cab. They thought they may be fighting or he may have been helping him in some way. They then reported that they witnessed the man wiping down the cab with some kind of a rag.

When it was discovered what had taken place, the police were called. Zodiac may not have intended for the crime to be reported this quickly as he had not had time to escape from the area.

When the call first went out over the police radio, for reasons unknown, the APB was for a black male. This could just be due to racism, an honest mistake, or (and most unlikely) someone working on the inside. Many have made different connections to the Zodiac and the police but nothing substantial. That doesn't mean their connections are not valid.

While on patrol, two police officers responding to the call would encounter an unknown white male who was walking away from the scene of the crime. This encounter would go down in the annals of Zodiac history. Officer Don Fouke and Officer Eric Zelms were said to have talked to this man and let him go because they thought they were looking for a black male suspect. In a later letter, Zodiac refutes this claim.

None the less, the officers gave a description of this individual that whether or not it actually was, became the face of the Zodiac killer.

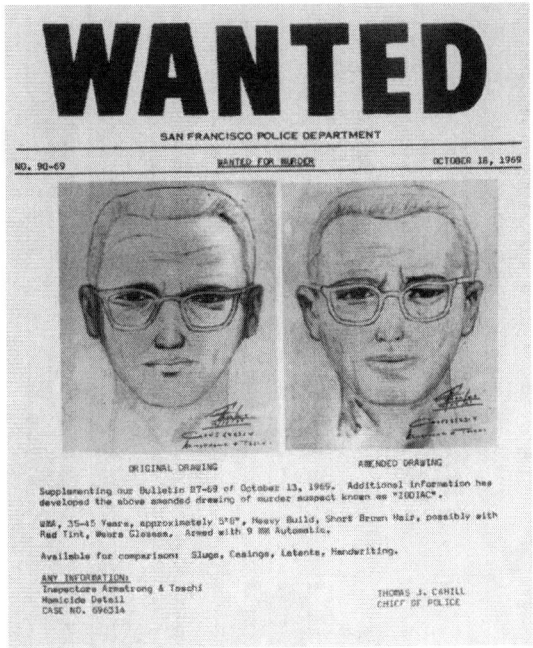

I created this full-body composite from the descriptions gave by witnesses.

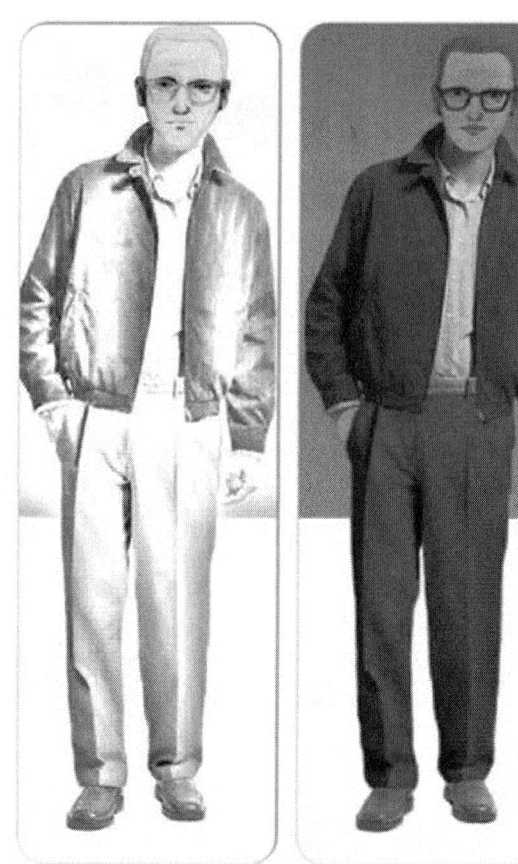

Whether or not this man was the Zodiac, or whether or not the officers actually talked to this man, may never be known. One thing is for sure, even though all of the stories have changed over the years, if you read the original reports made by these officers, and watch an interview done with them in the 2009 documentary "This is the Zodiac Speaking", someone is lying. You have to research it and decide all of that for yourself.

Again, people say this attack was a break in the Zodiac's

pattern. It was a single male that didn't occur at location lovers like to go for privacy. This is the fourth alleged attack by this individual. Maybe everyone is overlooking the real pattern.

All of the other attacks occurred near parks and golf courses. Every single one of them, and so did this one. Right down the street is the Presidio golf course and park. Witnesses said the man disappeared into the Presidio, a naval base in San Francisco. Zodiac himself claimed to have been hiding in the park beside the golf course in a letter he would send shortly after the crime.

This would be the last known attack by this individual and I stress the word "known". Because the only murders that were known to be committed by him, were murders he reported to the police himself. The police even admit they would have never connected these murders together if not for him. Other attacks would later be linked to him, but it is thought the man the police encountered that night was actually Zodiac because, in a letter that was mailed to the San Francisco Chronicle, the killer stated he would no longer announce his crimes. It is thought this close encounter may have rattled him.

One thing you can be sure of, he never stopped killing, he just stopped bragging about it. While all of these events were taking place, the killer mailed a plethora of letters and codes to the police and newspapers. In the next chapter, we will cover an overview of the letters and the dates on which they were mailed. This book is not intended to talk about murders and letters. It is intended to do one thing. To show how a mysterious blank map sent by the killer works. To show how it gives marked locations as well as highlighting the long looked for stretch of highway that Zodiac claimed to have planted bombs on. While it is unlikely that he really planted bombs on a stretch of highway, what better way to make sure people pay attention than with a bomb threat. While there is in all likely hood no bombs, there could something else important located at this place he wants us to find. As you will see, there was an actual place marked on this map. What, you may ask? Who knows, he did highlight this section of highway for a reason and for almost half a century this location has remained a mystery, until now. Since the world spent nearly 50 years looking for this stretch of highway, now that it has been found, you would think this would be of interest and paid attention to by investigators. Will anyone pay attention? Only you can make that happen.

To see full-color images of these crime scenes and other info, you can go to www.zodiackillerenigma.blogspot.com to view more of my work.

CHAPTER TWO – THE LETTERS

In this chapter, we are just going to do a brief overview of the letters sent by the Zodiac. To view the letters, you can go to www.zodiackillerenigma.blogspot.com .

1967, Riverside, California. A young college student by the name of Cheri Jo Bates left a note on the refrigerator in her kitchen for her father, Joseph Bates. The letter simply read, "gone to the library".

Cheri never knew it, but she would never see her father again. Upon reaching the library, a predator had waited for her to enter before accessing the engine on her Volkswagen Beatle and disabling the distributor. Removing the main wire on the distributor prevented the engine from starting.

The man then approached Cheri under the false pretenses of a friend and offered her help. In his letter he would later send to police, he would imply that he may have known Cheri and felt ignored by her.

It is thought that he pretended to try to fix the engine before giving up and offering her a ride. Luring her to his car which was parked around the corner by an abandoned house used by the library for storage, the man pulls out a knife and violently stabs her to death.

While it has never been conclusively proven this man

was the person who would later call himself 'The Zodiac', it is a pretty good chance that they were one and the same person. This is up to you to decide for yourself, but for the purposes of this chapter, this is where we will begin. I will provide thumbnails to give you some idea of what the letters looked like. I have a book with the full-size letters or you can view them online.

The Riverside Letters = 4-30-1967

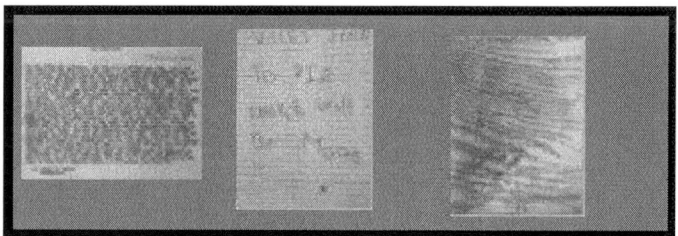

Two years later..........

After the July 4th attack of Michael Mageau and Darlene Ferrin, three Bay area newspapers would each receive a letter from a man claiming to be the murderer of Darlene Ferrin. He would also claim to be the murderer of David Faraday and Betty Lou Jensen the previous year. Each letter would contain one-third of a cipher later dubbed the '408 Cipher'.

The 408 Cipher Letters = 8-1-1969

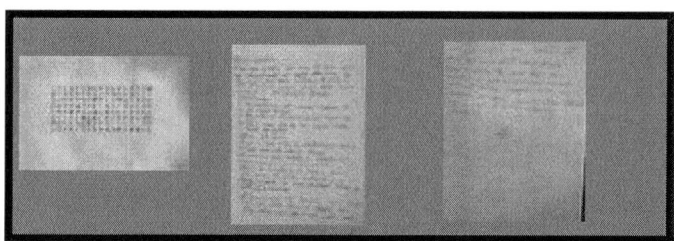

The police wanted to test the idea that this man was really the murderer of these people. So, in the newspapers, they sent this man a message asking him to send another letter providing more information about these murders. One mistake was made by the person who wrote these letters. He claimed that Darlene Ferrin had been wearing patterned slacks when in fact she had been wearing a patterned skirt. I have images of this dress that had been kept in evidence and recreated an image or Ferrin wearing the dress. It can be found on my site. This is an issue that has perplexed Zodiac researchers for years, but keep in mind that the attack had only lasted mere seconds, at night, in a high-stress situation. It is possible it was an honest mistake. The next letter we can call 'The Reply'.

The Reply Letter = 8-4-1969

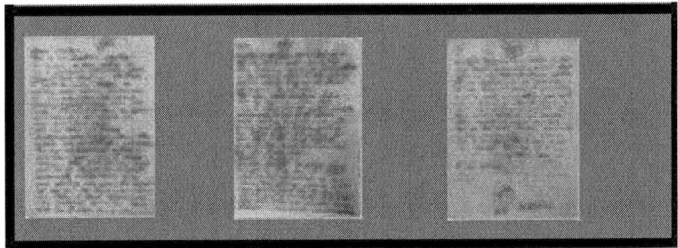

The next message from Zodiac didn't come in the form of a letter but was written on the side of Bryan Hartnell's car door after the Lake Berryessa attack. It was simply a circled cross with some dates written below followed by the words 'by knife'.

Hartnell's Car Door = 9-27-1969

The next letter would come after the murder of Paul Stine that occurred at the corner of Washington and Cherry Street in San Francisco, California. Near the Naval base called the 'Presidio'. This is the night that two police officers would claim to have had an encounter with a man who may have been the Zodiac and where the famous police sketch of the suspected killer originated. As proof that he was the murderer of Paul Stine, this letter would include a torn piece of Stine's bloody shirt.

The Paul Stine Letter = 10-13-1969

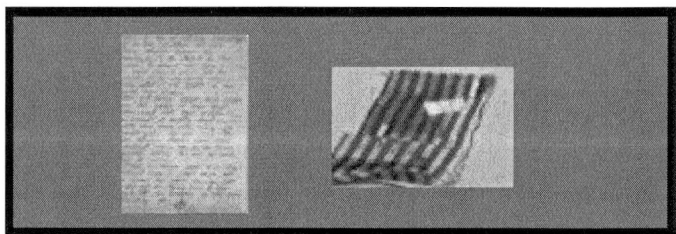

The next letter that was received from the Zodiac would probably be one of his most famous and infamous. It came in the form of a yellow greeting card with a fountain pen on the cover. The card would simply read, "I'm sorry I haven't written, but I just washed my pen". While washing fountain pens was an actual exercise that had to be done to maintain fountain pens, it is my belief that this has a veiled or double meaning. Zodiac did this often with clues. Besides a fountain pen, what other kinds of pens would you wash? Think of the famous peanuts cartoon character, Pig-Pen. We all know he was called Pig Pen because he was dirty and needed to be washed. A pigpen was also a form a cipher that was also known as the 'Masonic Code'. It had been used for centuries and was made from a key that resembled two tic tac toe boards with letters and dots. It was named Pig Pen in the olden days because the boxes that constructed the code from the keys reminded people of pens like you would keep a pig in. The inside of the card also had a message inscribed promising bad news, but it would be a while before we would get the news. Along with this card and message also came what would become Zodiac's most famous unsolved code, 'The 340 Code'. It is my belief that the bad news Zodiac had promised was hidden inside of this code, and we would not get it for a while because the code had to be solved in order to receive the bad news.

While this code is still considered to be unsolved, it is my belief that this code was really an overlay grid for a map that Zodiac would later send. The main purpose of this book is to discuss this map, not the 340 code. My first book goes into great detail about all of this. In an effort to simplify things and cut to what I feel is the most important thing I discovered about the map, I wrote this book which is much, much shorter. If this book sparks interest in anyone who wants to know more after reading it, you can either go to my site or find my first book (which has a few things in it that I did not want to put on the internet). We call this letter the Pen Card or 340 Cipher.

The Pen Card = 11-8-1969

The order and dates the letters were received are important and very important to my theory. After the alleged close encounter with police on the night of the Stine slaying, Zodiac claimed he would no longer announce any of his murders. Keep in mind, the only reason all of these murders were ever connected in the first place is because Zodiac wrote and claimed them. But after the Stine shooting, he stated he would no longer announce any of his murders. Still, he kept sending letters, why? Because I believe he had worked out a puzzle system in which he would mail out all of the pieces at different times.

On September 22, 1969, a nine-year-old girl would go missing. Her body would later be found near the Crystal Springs Lake and golf course. All of the other known attacks committed by Zodiac occurred near lakes, parks, and golf courses. I believe that among other things, the bad news Zodiac referred to could have been the unsolved murder of this little girl, who went missing a couple of weeks before the 340 cipher was mailed out and a month after Zodiac stated he would no longer announce any of his murders.

I discovered this unsolved murder only after investigating marked locations I found when I coupled the 340 code and the map sent by the Zodiac together. The exact location of this murder was marked by the very first dot in the 340 code. When I looked up the first location, I found the murder of this girl.

I only had the idea to couple the 340 code and the map after I discovered a "bomb drawing" was really and overlay key for the map and reading a clue in which zodiac promised another code he sent would reveal the location of a bomb when this code was coupled with the map. I put two and two together and that is how I came to couple the 340 code and the map. The main purpose of this book is to explain the coupling of this "bomb drawing" and the map. I will also discuss some of the other things I found also, but as I have mentioned, I have another book and a site that goes into great detail about all of this.

I created my site to post my work as I went along, no matter if I thought what I did was right or wrong. That was not the point, the point was to post all of my work for anyone to view and for me later to review and set aside the most relevant and important things I found which I later created into a book titled, "The Zodiac Killer Enigma". It was the end result of a ten-year-long project from which I gained nothing.

The dates of the crimes and letters are very important to my theory, as they show this murder of Susan Nason took place before the puzzle pieces were ever mailed and that the 340 code could not be solved without the other overlay puzzle pieces.

The next letter that was sent by the Zodiac was the first of two alleged bomb drawing schematics. He called this bomb drawing, "The Death Machine". It was a six-page letter with one page containing the actual bomb drawing. Also, written in the letter was a section he marked that was meant to be printed in the newspapers. This is important, as I believe anything, he asked to be printed had something to do with the bigger code. I have not figured out the use of this section and I may never. I also believe he may have hidden many codes in his letters. We call this letter, 'The Death Machine Letter'.

The Death Machine Letter = 11-9-1969

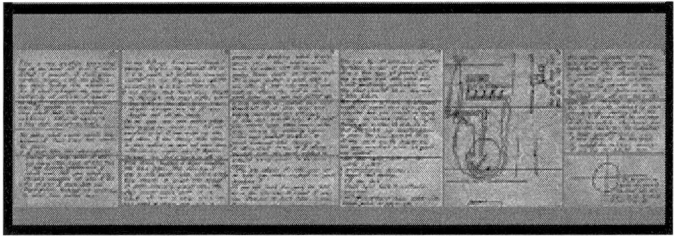

The next letter sent by Zodiac was to the famous attorney Melvin Belli. This letter was different in the way it was written. It was very neat and very straight. None of the other correspondences were written in this fashion. It is interesting that in two different sections of this letter, two words match each other in vertical positions. That is just something worth noting. We simply call this letter, 'The Belli Letter'.

The Melvin Belli Letter = 12-20-1969

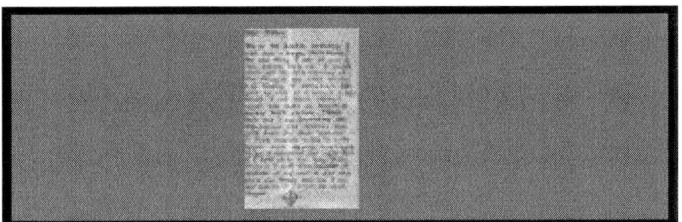

Four months later, Zodiac would send one of the other most important pieces to the larger puzzle. The second bomb drawing, which is not a real bomb drawing at all, but an overlay key for the map. The map itself, he had not yet sent. So, none of this could be put together. This bomb drawing also came with a "short" code that was dubbed, 'The My Name Is Cipher'. While I can not go into detail about this cipher in this book, I recommend either looking at my site or my first book. Part one is almost 500 pages long while part two (containing the letters and colorized, restored images of the crime scenes) is almost 300 pages long. They were meant to be published in one volume but publisher restrictions prevented me from doing so.

While this letter includes the bomb drawing, the world knows it as the, 'My Name Is Cipher Letter'. No one identified the bomb drawing as being important to the code before I did. The world thought it was just a bogus bomb threat and nothing more until I connected it to the map.

The My Name Is Cipher Letter = 4-20-1970

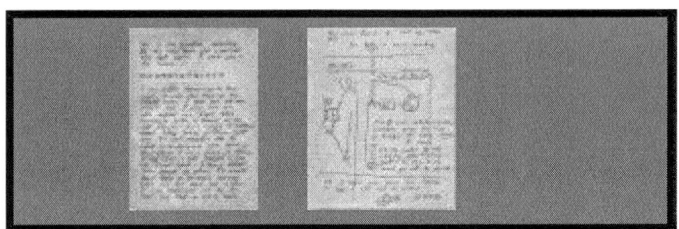

Eight days later the next letter was received. It was actually a pretty clever card which included some wordplay. The words, "I am sorry to hear your ass is a dragon" appeared on the front of the card. It is this card that made me think maybe Zodiac had some kind of inside information in the police department. If not, then how else could he have been so confident that their asses were draggin? Food for thought. We called this, 'The Dragon Card'.

The Dragon Card = 4-28-1970

Finally, we have come to the map. June 26, 1970, a section of a Phillips 66 map was received by Bay area newspapers along with what would be thought to be the last cipher sent by the Zodiac, but not the last puzzle. This code would be called the "32 Code' because of the 32 symbols comprising the code. It is in the letter with this code where the clue 'this code coupled with the map will tell you where the bomb is set. You have until next fall to dig it up". After discovering the actual bomb drawing itself can be coupled with the map to reveal a section of highway highlighted a string of bombs (all of which you will see shortly), I thought, map, bomb drawing, code, coupling. Since the bomb drawing can be coupled with the map, and he says a code can be coupled with the map, maybe the 340 code can be coupled with the map in an overlay just like the bomb drawing was. I mean, he did hint that "a" code could be coupled with the map. A lot of people have said to me, "Randall, this is wrong. The 340 code is not the code that was meant to be coupled with the map".

To which I reply, "How do you know that?"

To which they answer, "Because that is what the mass-murdering maniac, who has been caught lying, who has been caught giving clues while using misdirection at the same time told us. He said the 32 code, not the 340. I mean, he is such an honest guy, he has given us no reason not to trust him, Randall. You're wrong because Zodiac said so. You're just wrong."

To which I say, "So, he never told us the map could be coupled with the bomb drawing (and once you see it you will see there can be no doubt about it). He said his name would be revealed in the 408 cipher, was it? He said he was going to shoot off the tires of a school bus and never did, maybe he was trying to tell us something else with that comment? I can name a hundred other things. The 32 code could be used with the map in some way, in fact in my other book I show one way it can be and go into this more, but do you have to shut down the entire possibility that the 340 code has nothing to do with the map. He did give a clue that "a code could be COUPLED with a map."

They say, "The 340 code was sent before the map was ever mailed."

To which I say, "So was the bomb drawing that matches the map identically. It was also mailed before the map, but it matches it exactly. But I guess you're right. I mean, Zodiac did send these puzzles with no intention of them being challenging to solve and gave us explicit directions on how they were supposed to be solved and used. Oh, wait, no he didn't. That would negate the entire purpose of a puzzle and code."

I think you all can see where I am going with this. Some people will simply never accept it, and that is fine. They think that it means if I am right then they are wrong and that is simply not the case. I think all of these codes have more than one use because they are not just codes, they are also keys. I will never get that through the heads of some people, so I stopped wasting my time trying. In the end, it is up to you to decide. The police have already seen all of this and it is way too late to do anything about it. Still, it could help maybe find who he was at some point, that is why it should not be ignored. It may also help someone else besides me find other very important things.

You will still have to wait a bit to see all of this, but when you do, you will see there can be no doubt this bomb drawing is a perfect match in the map overlay. We will call this letter 'The Map Letter'.

The Map Letter = 6-26-1979

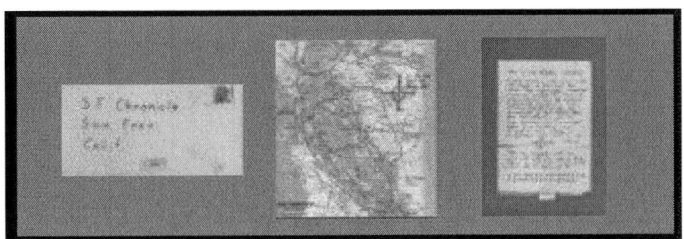

The next letter, we like to call 'The Kathleen Johns Letter'. Remember, Zodiac said he would no longer announce any of his crimes, but in this letter he did. Or did he? You see, Kathleen was assailed by a man she claimed was the Zodiac, but it is thought it really wasn't and Zodiac wrote this letter in response to a news story he read claiming he had kidnapped this lady and burned her car. Since the crime had already been blamed on him, he wrote a letter accepting that blame, but it is thought in reality, he had nothing "what so ever" to do with it. You just have to look into that and decide for yourself. For the purposes of this book, this letter has no bearing.

The Kathleen Johns Letter = 7-24-1970

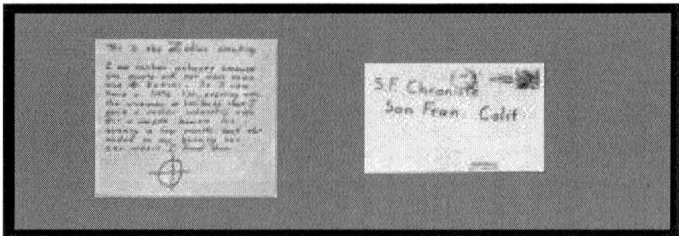

The next two letters which were both received at the same time two days later did contain clues that helped lead me to some of the overlay discoveries. I am not going to go into every clue in this book, as my first book covers all of that in detail. We call these letters 'The Little List and Buttons Letters'.

The Little List and Buttons Letters = 7-26-1970

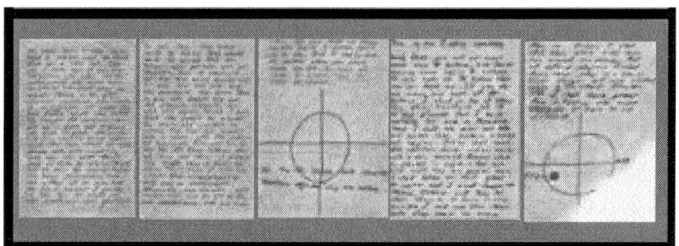

Next, we have what is referred to as the "Pace Card". In this card, Zodiac states that his pace has not gotten any slower and he gives us a new number of his victims. What makes this card interesting to me and my theory is that it has 13 holes punched into it with sections of text inverted. I believe this is a hint to the overlays.

The Pace Card = 10-5-1970

Now we have another card and not a letter sent by Zodiac. His famous Halloween card. This card I believe is also a hint to the overlays. I can connect everything on this card to the 340 code. EVERYTHING!!! You can see all of that in my other book or site, as it is quite a lot. Most of it you will see a little later. The Pace card featured 13 holes punched out in the card while the Halloween card has 13 eyes drawn onto it. It is possible that this card is some kind of overlay key itself that could be used somewhere to reveal some kind of hidden information. It could be used on a code or somewhere in the Zodiac letters themselves. All of the letters combined, form some kind of puzzle book. The puzzle book of a mad man.

One of the false ideas out there about the Zodiac is that this card came with a piece of Paul Stine's shirt. This is not true. It the 2007 film "Zodiac", Paul Avery can be seen opening the card to find a piece of Stine's bloody shirt. In reality, while the card was meant for Paul Avery (a San Francisco Chronicle Journalist who was said to be obsessed with Zodiac, though I don't believe he was obsessed) a piece of Stine's shirt was not part of the card.

That being said, it is thought that there could be other letters that were not released to the public that could have contained pieces of Stine's shirt. While this can not be conclusively proven, you can find info pertaining to this on Tom Voight's Zodiac site. I recommend it to anyone.

I do know there are letters that were never released to the public as my friend Richard Grinell of zodiacciphers.com conducts freedom of information requests for these letters all of the time. I also suggest checking out his work as it is very good and very detailed. Richard breaks down crime scene photos to reveal their scale and measurements. His work is quite impressive.

The Halloween Card = 10-27-1970

It would be five months later before the world would get its next letter or at least the next known letter I should say. The L.A. Times letter. This letter is the first sent by the Zodiac to a Newspaper in Los Angeles. On the envelope in large letters were written the words 'Air Mail'.

The L.A. Times Letter = 3-13-1971

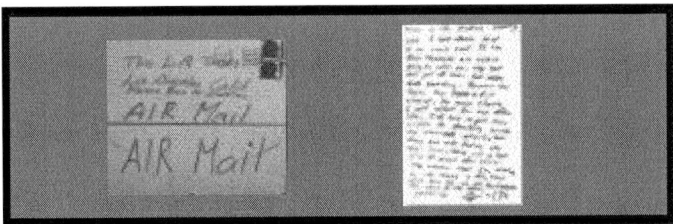

Next comes the Lake Tahoe Card. This card is reminiscent of the Pace card. As it also has a hole punched out in the card inside of a crossed circle and inverted text on the card. It is thought this card hints to a woman who went missing near the Lake Tahoe area at the time and gives clues to where her body may be. It features snips of an ad from a resort in the Lake Tahoe area.

The Lake Tahoe Card = 3-22-1971

The next letter, I find is one of his most interesting. It is in reference to a movie that had just come out that Zodiac had gone to see in theaters. You may have heard of it, 'The Exorcist'. He said it was one of the best satirical comedies he had ever seen. I think this statement gives us an insight into Zodiac. Only a person who was familiar with catholic dogma and exorcism would have known and saw the comedy in this movie. It scared the hell out of the rest of the world, but he saw the comedy in it. This was a time before the internet when this knowledge would have not been accessible to everyone. He implied he knew a little more about real exorcism than the average person. Did you know a real serial killer actually appears in this movie?

Also, at the end of this letter, there is an interesting puzzle. I call it a dot puzzle. There are a few interesting things about this puzzle. The first is that when you OVERLAY this puzzle on the envelope it came in, it matches the stamps on the envelope. Almost like he was screaming OVERLAYS at us. I will show you this overlay. Second, it matches a specific section of the 340 code. The very section that is used for the alignment with the map. Like the Halloween card, this puzzle can be connected with the 340 code and suggests that the 340 is to be used in an overlay. What are the odds of that?

The envelope overlay.

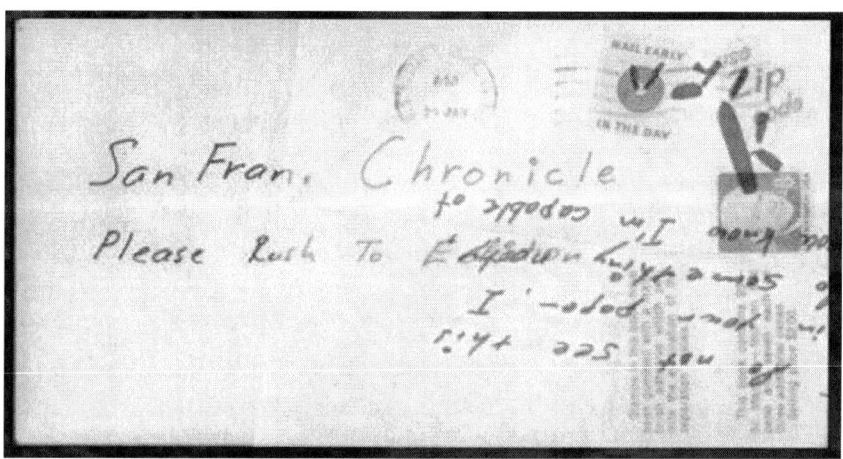

The 340-code match.

I go into detail about all of this in my other book. You can also find it on my site if you look.

I have to admit, only a working brain could have created that.

The Exorcist Letter = 1-29-1974

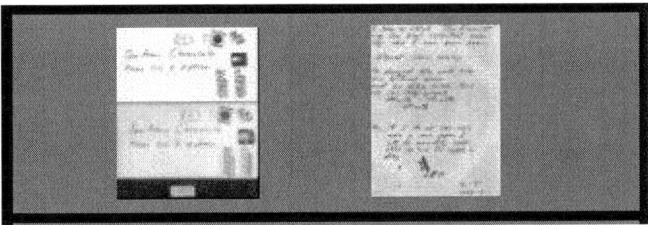

There are only a few letters left and they really have no bearing on my theory. It is arguable that a couple of them may have even been sent by the Zodiac, but they are associated with him. So, I will briefly include them.

The S.L.A. Card = 2-14-1974

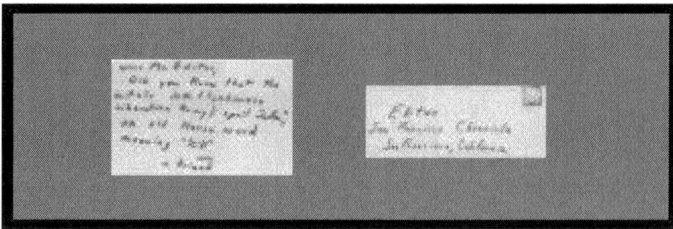

The Bad Lands Letter = 5-08-1974

This letter was also written about a movie called 'The Bad Lands'. A true story about a young couple who go on a murderous crime spree but make it into popular culture. If really written by Zodiac (and I have no reason to believe it wasn't) this may also give us an insight into Zodiac as it hints to his age and also places, he may be familiar with.

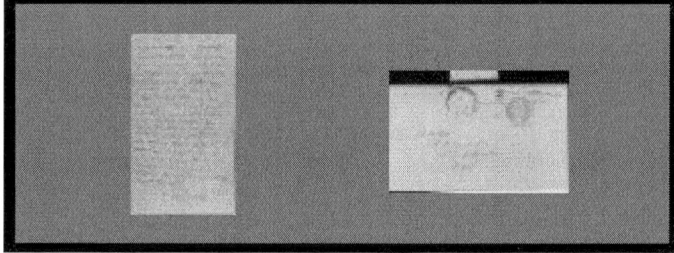

The Red Phantom Letter = 7-8-1974

The Christmas Card = 12-1990

In December of 1990, this card mailed from Washington State was received at the San Francisco Chronicle. Along with the card was a scan of two keys on a chain with an object that can not be readily identified and open to interpretation.

The card reads 'From your secret pal'.

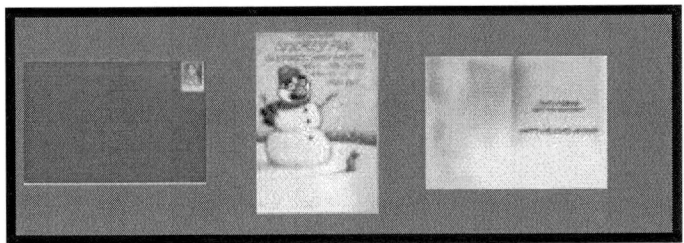

So, let's do a brief review of the letters and dates.

The Riverside letters	4 - 30 - 1967
The 408 Cipher Letters	8 - 01 - 1969
The Reply letter	8 - 04 - 1969
Brian Hartnell Car Door	9 - 27 - 1969
Paul Stine Letter	10 - 13 - 1969
The Pen Card & The 340 Cipher	11 - 08 - 1969
The Death Machine Letter	11 - 09 - 1969
The Melvin Belli Letter	12 - 20 - 1969
The 2cd Bus Bomb and The "My Name Is" Cipher Letter	4 - 20 - 1970
Your Ass is a Dragon Card	4 - 28 - 1970

The Map Code Letter	6 - 26 - 1970
The Kathleen Johns Letter	7 - 24 - 1970
The Little List & The Button's Letter	7 - 26 - 1970
The Pace Card	10 - 05 - 1970
The Halloween Card	!0 - 27 - 1970
The L.A. Times Letter	3 - 13 - 1971
The Lake Tahoe Card	3 - 22 - 1971
The Excorcist Letter Puzzle	1 - 29 - 1974
The S.L.A. Card	2 - 14 - 1974
The Bad Lands Letter	5 - 08 - 1974

The Red Phantom Letter	7 - 08 - 1974
The 1990 Christmas Card	December 1990

Chapter Three: Welcome to My World

Welcome to my world. Some time ago I made these discoveries about a puzzle the Zodiac Killer created and hid in plain sight inside of his codes and letters. Ever since I have been trying to show the world. This is not your typical book about the Zodiac. I am going to try a different approach. I am going to going to shoot it to you straight and convey all of this as a real person. A person just like you. I am going to explain how I got into this, the occurrences that led me to my findings, and all of the bullshit I have taken and gone through for simply trying to show it to people. I seriously doubt that there is anyone out there who has taken the approach to be real. I mean as a person.

My motivation for working on the codes was simply just because I found it all interesting. I have had some experience with such things over my life. So, when I found out about these codes, then I naturally had to take a look at it. I never actually expected to get anywhere with it, but when I did, then I had a choice. I could keep it to myself or I could share it with the world.

I started with trying to share what I found with the online groups and communities, but I to my surprise I was not received very kindly. This confused me. I did not have very much experience at the time with doing such things online and while some genuinely found my work amazing, others responded in anger, great anger.

I found an online Facebook group and I made my first post. The group appeared to have been inactive for quite some time. As I kept working and found more things I thought to be of interest, I would post them on this page one at a time. Over the course of a few months, I had made about ten or more posts. Most of which are covered in this book.

One day, I went to make another post and found that the group had blocked me. They overlooked what I was trying to show them and responded by making it clear that someone like me would not be tolerated in their group. As I did more work, I started finding the way people responded to what I was trying to do more interesting than the Zodiac codes themselves. This became an even greater puzzle to me.

My intentions were not to insult anyone or to devalue the work anyone else had done. I hoped they would take what I found and apply it with their own work. As I started looking at things other people had posted and how people had responded when others had come out making claims, I noticed that most of the time what these people did was ignored and that they were immediately attacked.

Still, I truly felt I had found something important that had to be seen. I struggled with it. On one hand, I had to show this to people who could maybe use it to find something bigger. What I was doing was not about personal gain what so ever. I have never really made anything from this project but it has cost me a lot. More than anyone realizes, but I made gains in other ways. On the other hand, I had to think about my family and any future family I may have. This worried me more than you could possibly imagine.

I didn't want the cruelty of some to affect the lives of my family. I am one thing, but my family is another. At first, I really was met with a lot of ridicule and dismissal, to the enjoyment of some.

After being blocked from this page, I felt disheartened. I did not want to go around the internet posting this stuff in groups and message boards only to be accused of spamming and such. My goal was not to argue. That was when I made a blog.

Surely, I could do all of my work and post it on my blog for anyone to see and then it could not hurt anyone. I could put it all there for anyone who wished to view it at any time they wanted to do so. I did what I could and put many hours into the project. I didn't have much to work with. An old laptop with no battery that someone had thrown away and I repaired. I had an old iPhone with a busted screen that I could use to make my models and images. Then I went around to online message boards and other groups. I would post a link to the blog telling people to check it out. That way I could not be accused of spamming because it was a lot to show people.

To my surprise, I was met with even more anger. Again, I was being banned and even more, some were personally tracking me down to put me in my place and call me a shill. A shill? Really? All I did was what the founder of Zodiac.com did. All I wanted to do was show it to people and share it with the world. I think some confused my motivations with their own.

I had seen people come out with books about the Zodiac only to be ridiculed with comments like, "well, if he was serious about this then why didn't he let us see it first before publishing it in a book?"

When I heard that I thought, "that is what I am trying to do. Share it with these guys". Then I guess if the person who wrote the book had shared it with the top people in the Zodiac community, would his work have been met with any different reactions? Also, would he have even gotten a publishing deal?

No one can say that I didn't try to share my work. I tried with great effort. While many people truly appreciated what I was trying to do, the establishment seemed to wish I would just disappear and be quiet. I am not saying anything derogatory about these people. They have done a lot for the case, but It became clear to me that none of these guys were ever going to listen to me. I wasn't trying to change anyone's mind about anything. I was just giving them a new angle, a new avenue to explore a subject that had long since gone stale. I thought about giving up, many times. It actually caused me great depression, and having my own internal struggles with depression and other things, did not make it any easier. I was the next thing to being homeless and working on the codes was one of the few things I enjoyed. It took my mind off the world and my problems for just a little bit.

To be honest, I had no idea what to do. So, I just kept working. An hour here and there at night before I fell asleep. I never liked to feel like I was wasting my time. Time is the most valuable thing you have in the world.

While this was going on, I was watching the community I live in fall apart. Jobs were leaving. Everyone was being laid off. Drugs had always been a problem in my area. I watched as meth started to come into my community and tear it apart. Then the people around me started dying. In three years, I lost seven of my closest friends. Some from an overdose, some from health, and more than I would like to admit by their own hand. Working on this was one of my only escapes from all of this. At least I was being productive and trying to do something positive.

Then when things seemed at their darkest, I received some encouragement from some people who I never thought or dreamed I would ever even get to talk to. I can not mention names, but they know and I know. That is all that matters. It was a real boost to know that real professionals had seen my work and actually believed I may be onto something. It was just the encouragement that I had needed, and that meant a lot to me after receiving such a hard time.

My blog was titled, The Zodiac Killer Enigma: Cracking the Zodiac Killer Code. My plan was to post all of my work, no matter what it was. I had to post it all, and then later explore each avenue. If one yielded fruit, then great. If one didn't, then leave it there anyway. Someone else may find it useful. Some would take some of the things I had said and try to use my words out of context against me. Still, I had to leave all of my work, no matter what it was. It was like an online notebook for anyone to view.

While I was doing this, I was also taking the most important things I had found and put them together in a book. I was working on putting all of this together when I saw a book published on Amazon under my tittle. This book was also endorsed by the same people who had blown me off. That is fine. I have no problem with that. I wish them the best. I would even try to help them if I could in some way. I don't see how all of us going at one another's throats is going to get us any closer to solving any of this. In fact, I am grateful to those people. They make it possible for new blood to get into the game.

Richard Grinell of Zodiac Ciphers. com was the first who accepted me as an equal and listened to me. I will never forget that. He even posted my work on his site. I had been reading his stuff for years and I held him in high regard. He is a very smart and talented man and it really meant a lot to me. After that, one at a time, more people began to listen. The major players still refused to even acknowledge me and I really didn't want to go where I was not wanted.

So, I kept working. I kept trying to share my work with people. I finished my first book and I worked on trying to get it published. I made a version that I had posted on Amazon. I also made a free PDF of that very same version along with the link to my site. I would go around to online message boards and such posting the map and bomb drawing overlay along with a link to Amazon and my site. I quite frequently would have a give away where anyone could read the book for free on Amazon. My motivation was not to make money, but if I could make a few dollars here and there then I think all of my hard work should be worth something. I didn't even have internet when I was doing all of this. I would create my posts and then later when I was at a place with Wi-Fi, then I would post it.

Even as recently as last week I posted the map and bomb drawing overlay on a message board along with a link to Amazon and my site. If anyone looked, they could find all of this for free. If they wanted to sort through it all to find all the good stuff or they could download a free PDF. Again, people went straight past what I had just shown them about one of the most famous unsolved mysteries of our age and wasted no time before calling me a shill. They missed the point and tore into me instead of thinking about what I had just shown them. That makes one wonder. I am not a person of means. I can barely afford to live, much less buy ads and spend money hiring people to help me. In ten years, I have made ten dollars from this and spent way more just trying to show it to people.

So, why do I keep doing this? Because one-day people will listen and will see the importance of what I am doing. It may be after I die, but it will happen.

I never got into suspects. My hope was that the establishment would use my work on their own suspects. Some have said that I named a suspect, but that is a lie. I may have had private conversations about possible names I may have found and pointed out, but I always made it clear that those names could mean nothing. That is up to the police.

My first book was over a thousand pages. I may not have gotten famous from it. I may not have gotten rich. It may not have been the best book ever written, and this one may not be either. No one can call it a failure. Just the fact I even wrote a book is a success. You would understand why if you knew more about my life. That is why I welcome ridicule, hate, and insult. The people doing it have no idea who or what kind of person they are attacking. They have no idea what I have been through in my life, they have no idea what I was going through when I was writing the book and doing my work. Doing the work helped grow as a person and that is my success. It opened the door to something positive in my life and to do more writing about other things. Each time I write something or create, I get just a little bit better.

Every day of my life is a struggle. I have to fight my own mind. I have to accept the daily reality of my life and surroundings. I have to deal with my depression and other mental struggles. I know at any minute as a recovering addict, that it could all slip away and I could relapse. I got clean doing this project. Opioids got the best of me, and a lot of others that were around me. That is hard for me to confess to you. I am not proud of it. I want to deny it and hide it from the world. But in that regard, doing this, even with all of the pushback I have gotten from some, I am a success. I changed my life for the better but I still have a lot of bad days. It is a lonely road for a recovering addict. While it does not help the reality of my community, while I see more and more people take their own lives as time passes, while all of it does weigh on me, this is one of the few things that's helps me escape all of that. All I want is for people to see what the Zodiac Killer map really does, and use it to find out what I cannot. I want to know. I have to know.

I am trying to be as real with you as I can. You are about to see something new and something real about a case that has had nothing new for a long time. Nothing truly real anyway. While it may not be new to some, it is new to

99.9999 percent of the world.

This is going to be an abbreviated version of what I discovered. You may have many questions, and somewhere out there you can find all of the answers. You don't even have to pay for them. Even if you did, I see nothing wrong with a man being paid for his hard work. While some may say shill, one could fire back by saying cheap, but I don't. All of that is beside the point. If you have something you want to tell the world, how do you do it without stepping on someone's toes? I wish someone would tell me because I don't have a clue. I am going to piss someone off no matter what I do.

My counselors tell me not to worry about people like that, just keep working and doing what you are doing, because no one else is going to and if some had their way then no one would ever know about any of this.

They tell me not to let the words of people I don't know, and even the words of people that are close to me, bother me. They tell me that people are not there to see what you are doing and what you have to struggle with. Most of the people I am close to don't have a clue I am even doing any of this.

As time goes by, I will become a better writer. I will become more experienced in the processes of how all of this works. I may even accidentally write something that everyone will love. Who knows? I know what will happen if I do nothing. Sometimes I feel like just walking away from all of this, but deep down, I know I never can. You can't swim against the current. You can try but you will only die tired. It is like trying to run from an Apache attack helicopter. I don't know where this all will lead me, but good or bad, I have to go with it.

So, here is how it all started..........

Chapter Four: The Zodiac Overlays

Once upon a time, on a couch far, far away……...

There was a guy who was sitting alone way up in the Appalachian Mountains of Eastern Kentucky. Watching a movie called Zodiac just after his father had passed away when something caught his eye.

He had only caught a glimpse of it, but he could clearly see the strange symbols mapped out on a white sheet of paper.

"I have to show this to Mo", he thought.

After convincing his friend to come and take a look at this strange writing that appeared on this paper in this movie, they talked about it for a bit.

"You mean no one has ever solved this?", his friend asked.

"The hell if I know but not as I am aware.", I replied. "Do you think we could find a copy of it on the internet? It looks like some of the stuff we did growing up and something we would be into."

"Yeah, we could probably find it on the internet. Just one problem, the only place around here that has the internet is at the library. Every time they try to expand the internet out here some politicians will say, 'Noooo. We can't have the hillbillies actually getting educated'." (I hate politicians)

"Well, I guess we are going to take a trip to Jackson or Hazard."

And then I got my first good look at the Zodiac 340 cipher.

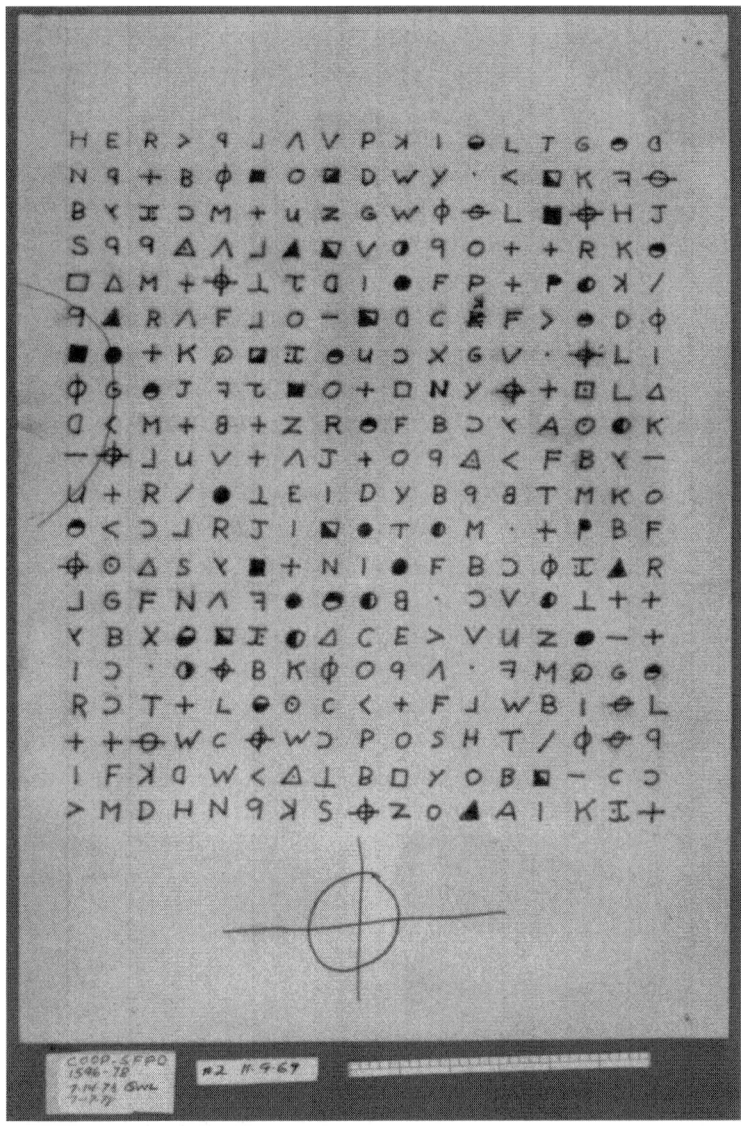

After about a year of trying hundreds of different approaches to solving this code and getting nowhere, I decided to watch the movie again.

"THE LETTERS!!!", I thought. That is why no one is getting anywhere solving this thing. Surely, he had to have hidden clues or some kind of key in his letters. That is quite common when it comes to solving, creating, or sending a code or secret message. I go into the history of this in my other work and show quite a lot of examples. Keep in mind, this book is meant to be a shorter, cheaper version to make it easier for readers to acquire.

When people did actually read my first posts online, they would say, "He is not showing his work, it's too simple. It can't be that simple. Not for a genius like Zodiac. This has to be a hoax."

I can promise that it is no hoax and why anyone would idolize this guy or think he is a genius is beyond me. It's like writing and playing an awesome song on a guitar. It is easy for the writer because he is the one writing it, but for someone listening to it for the first time, it may seem almost impossible for them to learn and play without any direction of any kind. Because it came from the head of someone else.

It took me about a year to do it all, but I went to the library and other places and I would print off copies of the letters here and there. I would study each one as I printed it off and then I would put it in a binder. That is what the second part of my first book is. The Zodiac letters. It also has restored colorized images of the crime scenes and other things for someone to acquire if they wanted a quality solid copy of the letters on paper, but I think it is important not to look at the code as one thing or a particular letter as one thing. You have to look at them all as one thing. As pieces to a larger puzzle. Codes could be and probably are hidden all over the letters just waiting for someone to discover them. They are not just a group of letters; they are a puzzle book of a mad man. That was the one thing I had done differently that no one else had ever thought to do.

Over time I studied the letters an hour here or an hour there. Usually, as I was lying in bed about to fall asleep. That seems to be when my mind is the most active and when I need the most to relax.

I started noticing a pattern of clues forming, so I made note of them. I then identified all of the most important pieces of the puzzle and made copies of those to keep together in one place. That was the step that led to the accident that started all of this.

Identifying all of the codes. Well, it didn't take a genius to do that. They were quite plain. But after putting them all together and looking at them side by side as one and comparing them with the pattern of clues; things started jumping out at me.

The very first thing that jumped out at me was that the 340-code looked like it was meant to be split into four quadrants. That was when I saw it. something no one else in the world had ever seen before. They were numbered.

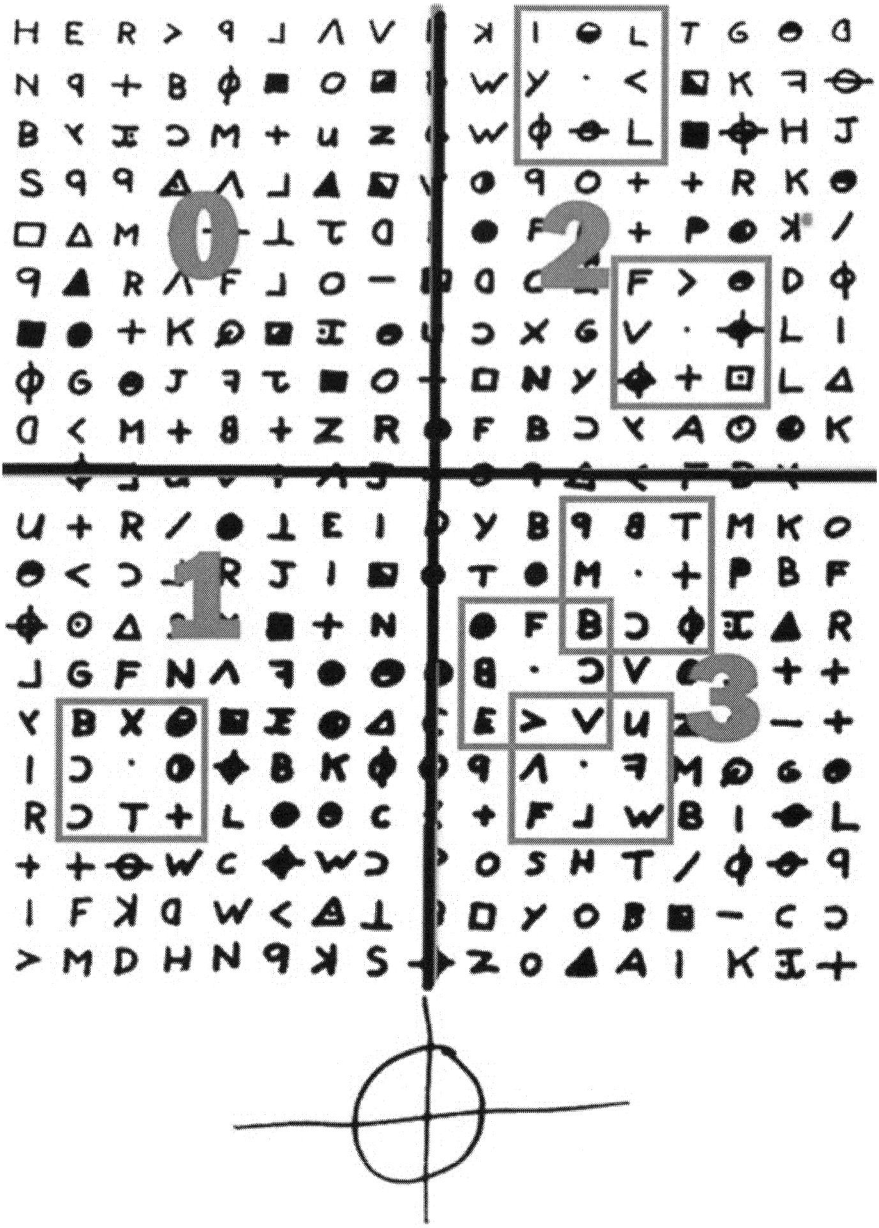

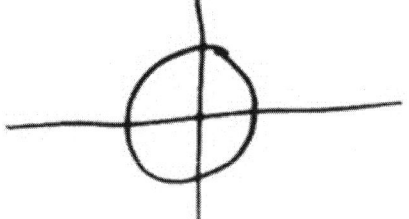

Those dots had always bothered me. One of the things that one can do in solving a code is to attempt to identify the things that seem to not belong. Those definitely do not belong. You have to admit it, and Zodiac never used them in any other code.

There is quite a lot going on here with those dots and that code. I didn't know it yet, but those dots did more than just number the four quadrants of the 340-code. Quite a lot more, and still more that I can not figure out. That is one of the reasons I feel it is so important that people see this. Someone who knows more than I do may see this and know exactly what it is that I was missing. It has something to do with navigation skills.

There was another very important thing that these dots played a part in on this code that I would see later. First, I had to make my next discovery. I was showing this to a friend one day when I had all of the puzzle pieces laying out on the floor in front of me.

I had two very important pieces that I didn't even have any idea were connected to one another. I had no idea that one piece was even a piece of the puzzle. I had my suspicions about it because of something I had seen once when I was in elementary school. A place called Caney Elementary. It was a very small school in the middle of the mountains that had been built over a hundred years ago.

First, let me show you the piece. This bomb schematic sent by the Zodiac. It is not a real bomb schematic at all, but something much more.

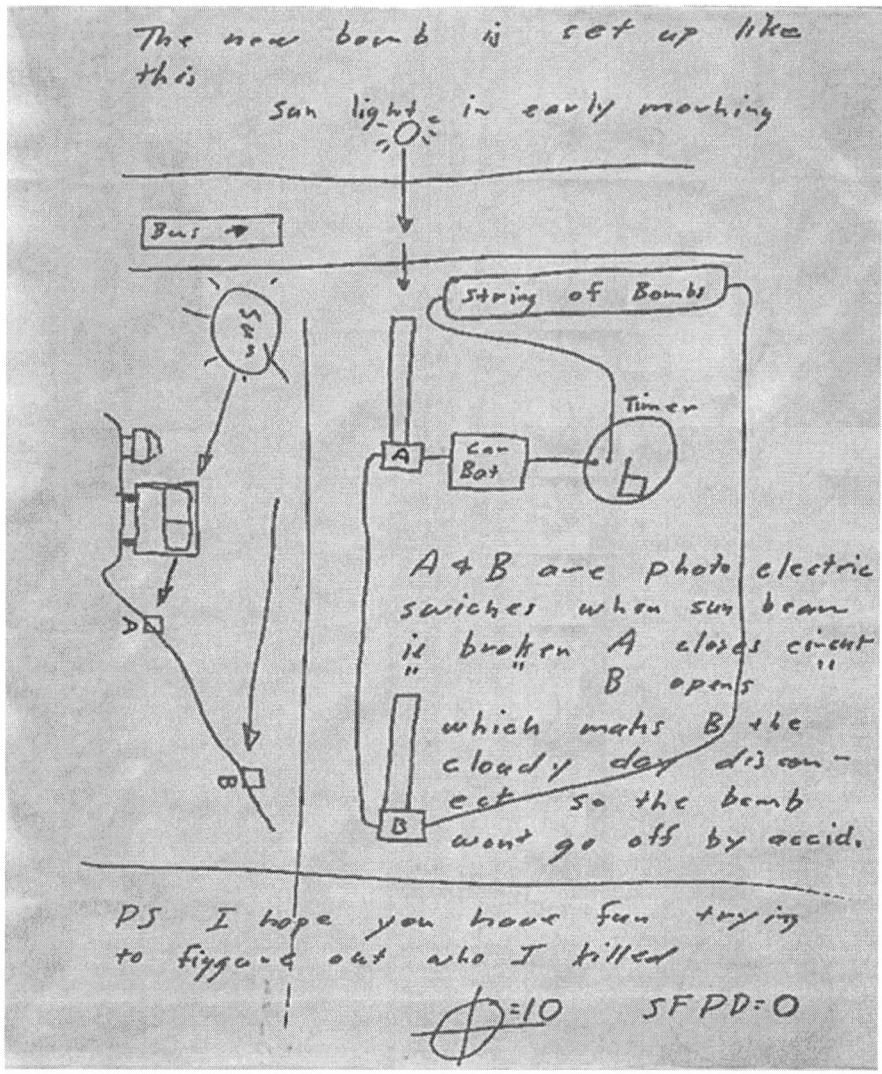

When I was a small child while in class one day, the teacher said we were going to make hidden messages. First, we were told to draw boxes on a blank sheet of paper, just like the boxes in the image above. We were creating something called a 'Cardan Grille'.

Then we were told to use a second sheet to overlay over the first and write a message to one of our friends inside of these boxes.

After that, we were instructed to hide the boxes by drawing a picture around them, just like in the image you have just seen. Then we were instructed to hide the message by writing a letter around it.

This was something that was very well known and surprised me that no one had ever considered before. I mean, at least as a possibility. Come on?!?!

Codes like this have been used for hundreds and hundreds of years. They were really quite popular in the American revolutionary war.

Watch a show called Washington Spies. You can find it online. It is about the spy ring George Washington ran during the Revolutionary War. You will see this process used quite a bit.

I found a Christmas card that used this process also that was created around a hundred years ago by one of the most famous cryptologists in American History, William Friedman. I reference his work a lot and use them as examples in my first book. I show more than ten different ways the 340 can be used based on his work.

Here is what his card looked like. You placed the grille over the code and turned it to reveal a hidden message. This is one reason I say messages could be hidden all over the Zodiac letters and codes. You don't have to focus on just one code.

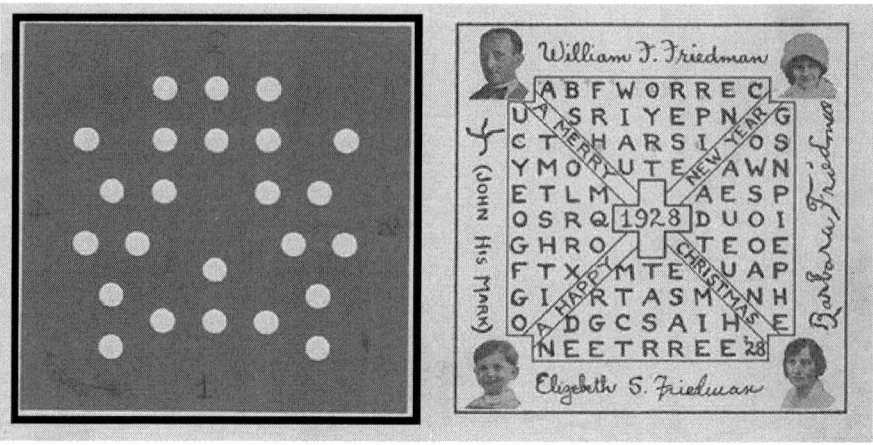

Back to the story. I had that bomb drawing and the Phillips 66 map that was sent by the Zodiac lying beside one another.

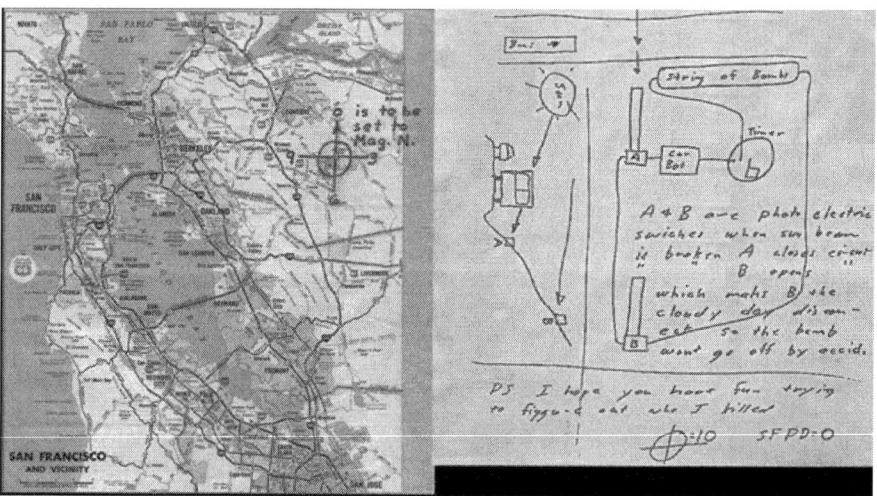

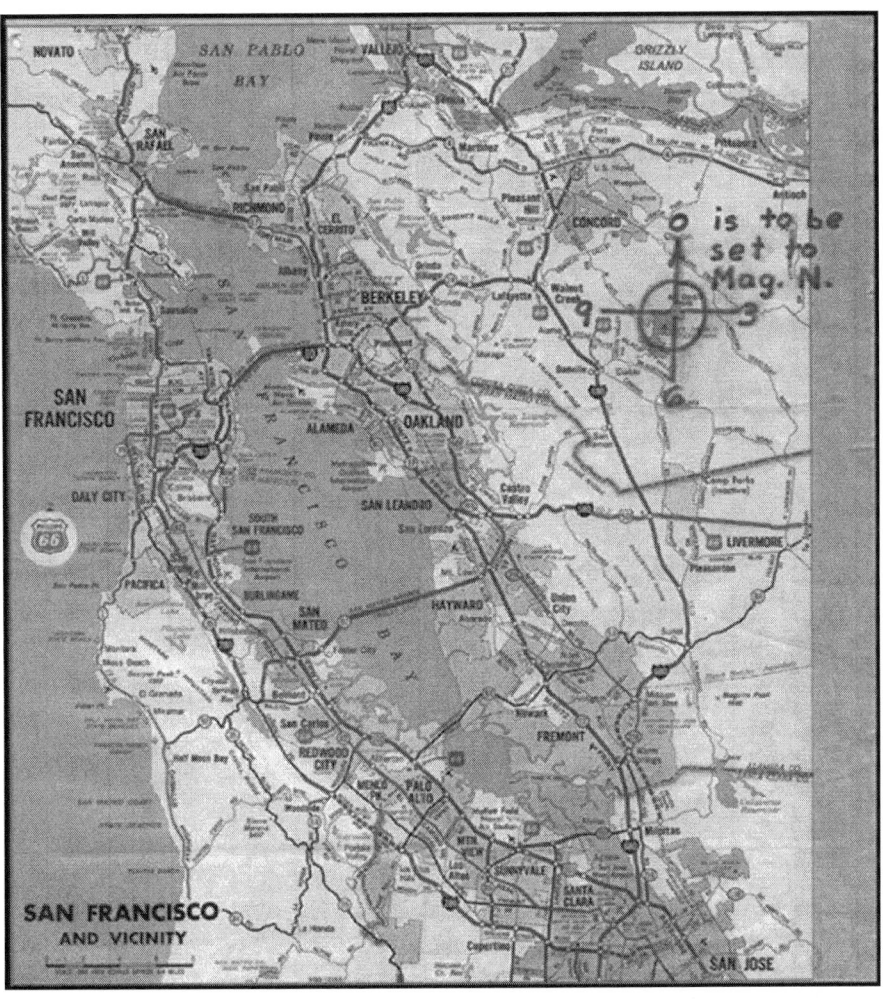

Before I point it out, see if you can notice what it was that caught my attention on your own. Study it really closely and see if you can notice all of the similarities between the map and the bomb drawing. For decades, no one had a clue what this map was or could be used for. Most didn't even consider it part of the code even though Zodiac said it was. While I was mostly ignored, after I came out with this many people did have their own spin-offs. Look for yourself and you can see the time frame of all of this. I found this in 2013-14.

Let me point out the most obvious similarity first.

The compass on the map and the timer on the bomb drawing. Those were the first two things that caught my attention. I never would have noticed this if I had not had them side by side. It was a complete accident.

After looking at this very closely, I noticed something else that seemed to be very interesting. Notice in the bomb drawing that there is a section with a bus and a car drawn onto it. In the bomb drawing, this is supposed to represent the side of a hill with the bus and car on a highway.

This is actually a clue. First of all, 'think bus and car on the highway'. Now think, 'side of a hill'. I do not live in California but the entire world knows that San Francisco is famous for its homes built on the hills next to the ocean. So, what is this section of the drawing with a bus and car on a highway next to a hill? It is actually a section of highway that runs through San Francisco. Far Fetched? Look closely.

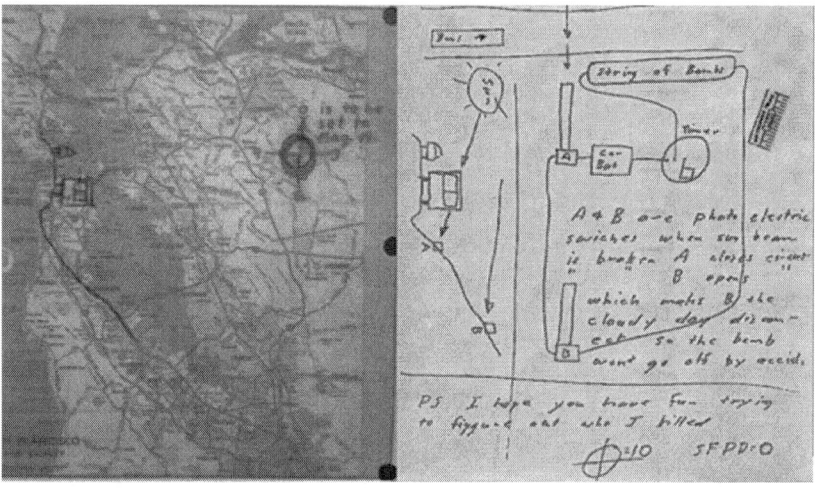

That is the copy I was using the day I noticed it. When you overlay these two documents onto one another and align the compass on the map with the timer on the bomb, they are an exact match.

Notice the points on the bomb drawing marked A and B. These could be marking actual locations on the map. You would think that people would be excited about this. I mean, you would think the establishment would be, which I am not a part of.

"A" marks a location near a cemetery. There could be something else important there. I don't know. That is why it is important that people who can find out more about this, see it.

The location that is marked "B" however, is a little more exciting. Keep in mind that this is a threat against a school and that the map was promised to give the location of a bomb. Whether there was a bomb or not is beside the point. People focus too much on whether there really was a bomb or not and miss the other possibilities. It could be something else, like a dumping ground, hunting ground, body, or even a real bomb that was never detonated or discovered. It could be his home. That would be really explosive. You would think people would want to know the answer to these possibilities.

The section marked "B" marks an actual school, exactly on the map. I talk a lot about this in my other works. You can try this for yourself. The map has a scale marker and a police photo of the bomb schematic also has a scale marker. I invite anyone to try this experiment for themselves. You can either print out the models I have already made or create them yourself. Either way, you will get the same result if done correctly.

As I stated earlier, when I made my first posts on my site, I kept it simple so no one would be confused. That was when some attacked it as being too simple and complained that I didn't show my work. They said I didn't prove the scale of these documents and they laid out a complex argument about why it was all wrong.

It amazed me that as much as some had claimed to know about and be familiar with all of this, and how much some claimed to be expert on this stuff, that they completely missed these two scale markers right in front of them printed on both documents. A pencil and piece of paper used on the screen, and they could have solved their own objections. I thought they would. I chalked it up to an honest mistake. Still I wondered how they missed that, or maybe they didn't miss it and just hoped that like a random political meme on the internet with some inflaming words pasted onto it, that people would read their comments about scale, agree, and move on while not noticing the scale was actually already on the documents.

You would think experts would already know this being so familiar with it and being, you know, experts, and if it was an honest mistake then that opens up even more questions. Ok, they took a poke and me and right now I am poking back. In reality, I am a very polite person, until given a reason not to be.

Still, I addressed their concerns about it all being too simple. I wanted to keep it simple to make it easy for anyone to understand. It wasn't written for just the die-hards who wanted a complex explanation with all of the details.

So, I starting making posts that had shown every step I had taken. I showed the proof of the scale of all of these documents and laid it out in such a way that no one could argue with it. Then I posted it.

Then the very same people who said it had been too simple were saying it was now too complex. There was no way it could be that complex and that it all looked forced together. Well, that was just laughable. That was when I realized that no matter what I did they were never going to look past their own ambitions and see what I was trying to show them. First, it was too simple and then it was too complex. I still got messages from people calling me a shill for doing nothing more than saying, "Hey, look at this". Maybe if one of their own had come up with it, then they may have listened. But who was I? Just some guy who wasn't part of the establishment. A nobody that no one had ever heard of. I am just a person, just like you. I put my pants on one leg at a time, just like everyone else. A smart person would have taken what I had shown to them and said, "Hey, look what this guy did. I wonder if it has any connections to any of our suspects? Or at least scrutinized it. What if this is the key that is missing in all of my own work? We should look into this and see how it may apply to the different theories and suspects of our own. This could open new doors for us!!"

But not a single damn one did, as I am aware of. As I tried to show more people what I had discovered, they then shifted focus from the map to say, "We looked into your suspect and nothing was there. It's time to turn the page." No shit, more than one actually sent me correspondences stating that.

Again, it is just another way of saying, shut up and disappear from the establishment. What suspect? I never had a suspect. I made it clear in everything I had done that I wanted nothing to do with a suspect. I am a code and puzzle guy. I can point out possible names inside the codes, and if people exist with those names, then there is nothing I can do about that. I never said anyone with those names was the Zodiac killer. How could I possibly know something like that? It does give establishment guys new avenues to explore. Let's say a name is found in the codes and was meant to be there. Why would you jump straight to, "It's the name of the Zodiac!!" There could be many reasons Zodiac could have put that name in there. It is just something of interest. That is all. People will put words in your mouth and love to do so. You will notice I have not mentioned the names of anyone nor spoke ill of anyone.

To do so does none of us any good and all of the people who are working on this case are important. No one working on this case should be blindly dismissed out of hand. I have always told people to be careful about names because you are either harassing innocent people or messing with a serial killer. Both are stupid ideas.

Richard and others had told me some would try to do that. That is why I won't even talk about possible names anymore, even in private conversations. Some just want to find any way they can to discredit you, cuts into their cash flow. That's just the truth of it. It was always funny to me how ordinary people could get it, but the establishment seemed to be so combative and unwilling to see it. Or maybe they just don't want to. I am sure I will get some shit for this later down the line, but anyone with eyes can see the map and bomb drawing were designed to be used in this manner. You would have a better chance of winning the lottery three times over than for this match between these two documents to be a coincidence. No matter what I do, I fear they will never accept it simply because of who found it. The truth is, some don't want the case solved while some believe so much in their suspect, that they would never accept that anyone else committed the crimes. That being said, there is nothing wrong with their convictions.

For example, if the authorities were to arrest someone right now and had incontrovertible evidence and DNA this person was the Zodiac, and this person was someone they had never heard of, there would be a large number of people who wouldn't accept that. I mean, one can understand why, but what I am doing has nothing to do with a suspect. It can be used and applied to every suspect to find any connections. One person told me, "of course, someone is going to get mad when you told them they just wasted their life." I never told anyone that, but he said my work implies that. No, it doesn't. Their own insecurity implies that.

So, look at the overlay with your own eyes and decide for yourself. Here is a quality image of the bomb drawing and map overlay for you to study.

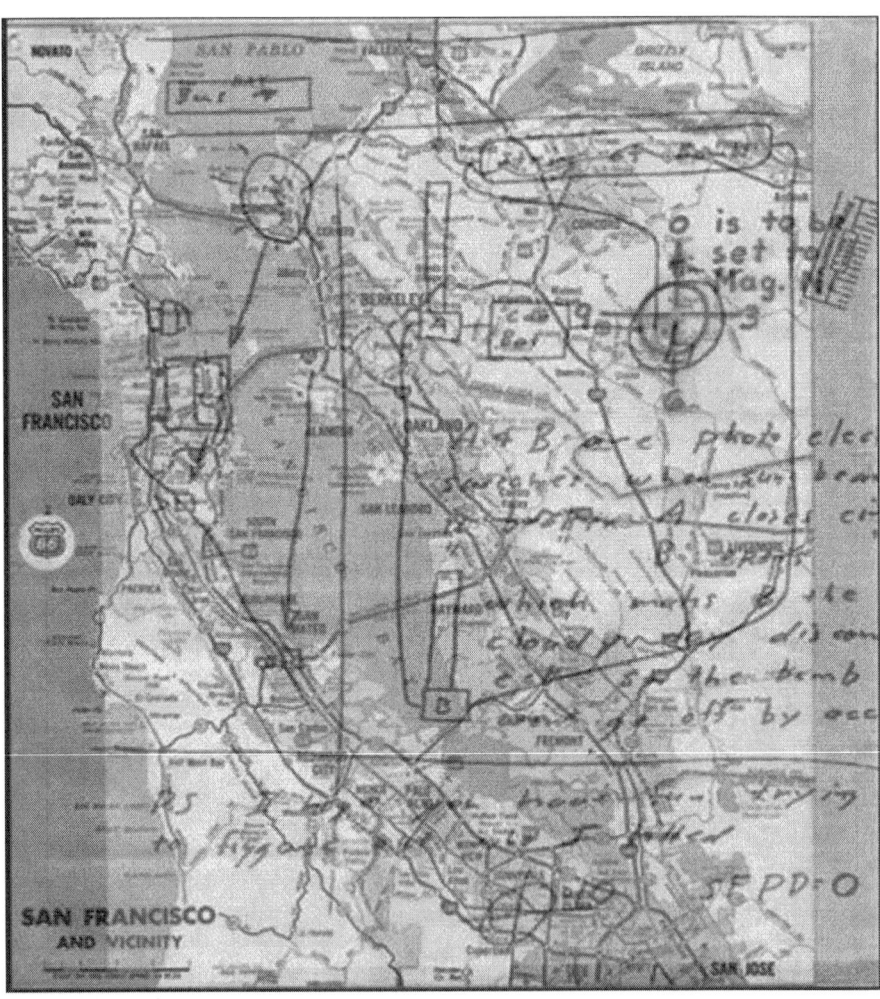

At this point, I want to show you some closeups of this image and some of the most important parts you need to take note of. You may also find things that I missed. People find things all of the time that I missed and point them out to me. That is my motivation. Teamwork. That is why it is so important that people see this.

First, let's look at the section of highway running through San Francisco. The army manual on preparing map overlays (because this technique is taught in the military) says that a map overlay must have two points on opposite sides for the alignment of the overlay. If not then you would not know how to align the overlay. I believe the section of highway (while being part of the overlay that marks locations) is one of these two points for alignment while the compass and timer are the other markers.

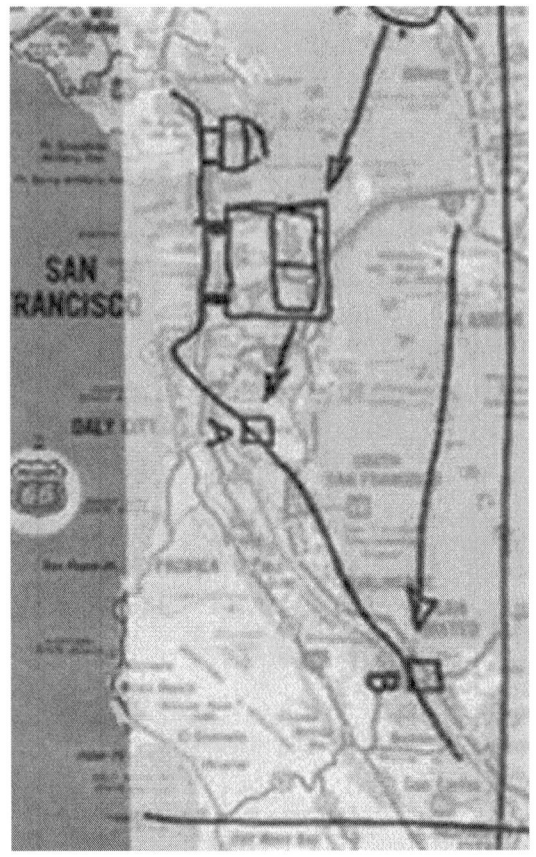

Let's also look at a close up of the timer and compass overlaid on one another. Here are both markers and points for alignment. What are the odds that this was an accident or coincidence? It can only be by design.

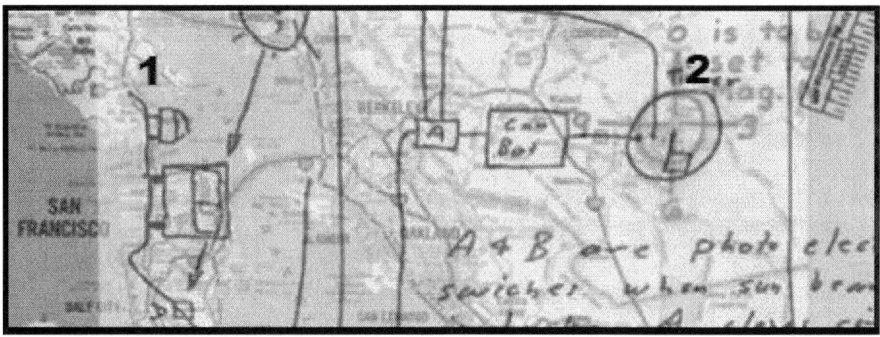

So, if they are used for the alignment, what exactly are they aligning to show us? While points "A" and "B" give us marked locations, this overlay also gives us one very, very important marked location (and probably more that are yet to be noticed).

Remember, this all revolves around a bomb threat against a school bus. Whether there was a bomb or not is irrelevant. The mystery is that Zodiac said this map could be used to find a marked place where a bomb is alleged to be buried. What the real meaning of all of this is, is what we must figure out. Here it is, the most important information hidden in this overlay code. Study it. Zodiac said, there is a section of highway marked by a string of bombs. Bomb or not, something important is at this location. You would think everyone would want to know what?

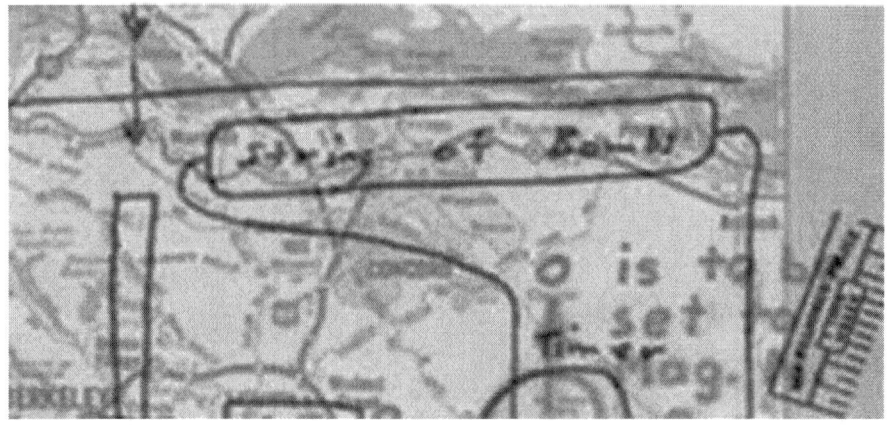

There it is, a string of bombs highlighting a section of highway found using the drawing of the bomb itself. Why else would he have sent this bomb drawing? It wasn't just meant to scare people. It had an actual use and I just showed it to you. Remember, we all know Zodiac was all about codes and hidden messages. You can try this experiment for yourself. Some will still dismiss this and come up with a thousand reasons it should be ignored. The question you must ask yourself is, why do some want this to be brushed off so badly? What is the harm in studying it? Seriously, give me one damn reason hard proof should be ignored while a thousand other ideas with no hard proof should be accepted? Think about that. Why dismiss this?

I cover this overlay in detail in my first book, but I want to include a small sample of what the army manual on preparing map overlays says about how to label a location with bombs on a map overlay. I want you to compare the excerpt from the manual to the bomb schematic overlay.

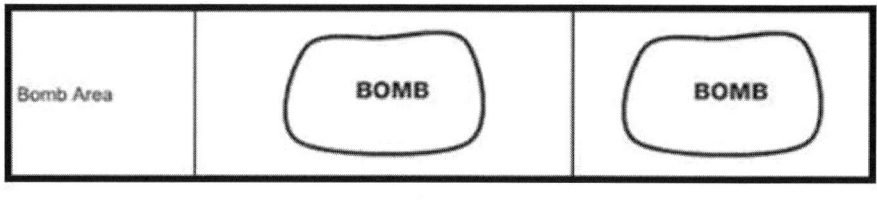

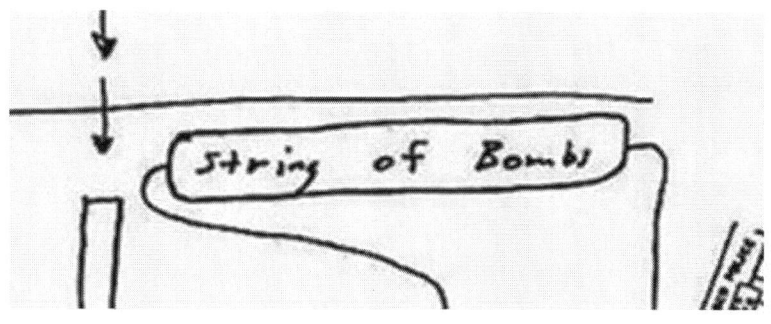

A simple circle with the word bombs written inside of it. I have the entire PDF of this army manual on my site and my first book. It supplies a sample overlay that shows what it would look like. You can find the web address or link to the site at the beginning of this book or you can read my first book which has all of the best stuff all together so you don't have to sort through mountains of information. It also includes some things not found online, anywhere. It includes many things that may also be of interest in relation to this method.

While we may not know who Zodiac was, we can use his letters to identify things about him. Such as personality traits, things he found of interest, the kinds of life experiences he may have had that led him to his activities (such as code making and overlaying), etc....

We can also use the letters and codes to identify certain words and phrases he used that may lead us to other insights about who he may have been. A certain word or phrase may lead us to the region in which he lived or where he may have originally been from or grown-up.

I believe Zodiac may have lived a life of privilege. That is not to say that he was super-rich, but he had the means and access to things that others may not have had. I believe he had some type of issue with jealousy and women. He felt entitled yet subjected. He had a very active imagination coupled with the boredom and anger that led him to act out in the ways he did. Such as murdering innocent people, bragging about how smart he was, and testing his intelligence compared to others with the creation of his codes. It was probably some sort of exercise that made him feel like had some sort of control over his life that he had felt like he had lost or never had. It made him feel good about himself.

He was well educated, despite his grammar and misspelling of words. I believe some were honest mistakes while most were done on purpose. Either to direct or misdirect us in some way. Grammar has no bearing on actual IQ. Everyone is an expert on something in their own way.

I believe he had an interest in the occult. Whether he actually believed in such things or not is another question. You do not have to actually believe in something to be interested in it. I believe this interest expanded into other areas like secret societies and symbolism which itself extended into cryptology or cryptography.

He did make references to things that your average person would not have known. This indicates he had some exposure to it. Identifying things that he had said, referenced, or hinted to that an average person may not have known is one of the keys to discovering who he actually was.

For example, the crossed circle that he liked to sign his letters with. This could have originated in many places. Most know about the Zodiac watch and that it used a crossed circle like that of a gun sight as its logo. Some believe this is where he stole it from. That may or may not be so. While I do believe he probably had knowledge about this watch and maybe even owned one, no one ever asks where and why did the watch company use that name and logo for its watch.

The Zodiac, the celestial zodiac, was one of the first tools man used to keep track of time and the seasons. Time…... The crossed circle was used by many cultures as a way of tracking time and seasons over the calendar year. It became a sacred symbol in many cultures. In my first book, I reference an article by the Free Masons on this very subject.

I am not going to get into the history and origin of the Christian cross, except to say it had other origins than just something that Christ was crucified on. The cross was used by many cultures. I want to mention this because I am going somewhere with it. The Celtic cross also resembled the crossed circle used by Zodiac. Zodiac also makes hints and references in his letters to Celtic beliefs and practices. This could be that he had an interest in cultures that had assimilated some Celtic beliefs into their own dogma over time.

Another group that holds the crossed circle in high regard is the Catholic Church. I want to point this out because it may be helpful to someone at some point. This is because he makes more than one reference to things associated with the Catholic Church. Just as he hides references to the Free Masons and secret societies. The square and compass are one of these references that he hides as clues in different places.

One of these references to the Catholic Church comes in what we call the Exorcist Letter. While exorcism is used by more than one sect of religion or Christian denomination; the most famous (and the one used in the movie) is the Catholic church's views on exorcism. In his letter, he stated that it was one of the best satirical comedies he had ever seen. Only someone who had been familiar with the church's real views and practices on exorcism would have seen the humor in the movie. In other words, while the movie scared millions of people into going to church, he saw all of the bullshit used in the movie to make more frightening. He found it humorous. Suggesting he had some experience with the Catholic Church and its views on exorcism, and took pride in that he knew how it really was while millions were frightened by it. For example, drug addiction is a real demon to millions of people that manifests itself in the weakness of the human condition. I could write a book just about this subject.

He made another reference to the Catholic Church

many, many times. This reference was right in everyone's face, yet no one saw it. It came in the form of one of those misspelled words I was just talking about. Or was it misspelled?

In his letters and cards, Zodiac used the word 'Christmass" many times. He always put an extra letter 's' at the end of the word. Everyone considered this to be a misspelling he had done by mistake because he was poorly educated and had bad grammar. Others thought he was just playing with the word. In fact, the word 'Christmass' with and extra 's' is an actual word. It is used by only one group in the world (as I know of). The Catholic Church. Christ Mass. During the Christmas season, the Catholic Church will hold a Mass for Christ. Maybe none of this means anything. Maybe it means everything. You have to keep yourself open to all of the possibilities or you will find yourself hitting a dead end with nowhere to go very quickly.

So, you have just seen the most important discovery I made. If no one pays attention to anything else I have said or done, it would be a mistake to ignore that. The bomb drawing is used with the map. That is now a proven fact but decide for yourself.

You would think that marked locations on a map sent by a serial killer would excite people. It is like a treasure hunt in some ways. Almost like a real-life Da Vinci Code. All you have to do is look. Who knows what you may find? While it may not be a bomb, I can guarantee you that it leads to something. Real adventures are few and far between in reality.

One can only wonder what it is about these places that made them important enough to hide in a map code that went undiscovered for fifty years. Look at the section of the road marked by the string of bombs. While this overlay leads us to this rather large area, there are probably other things hidden in the letters and codes that could lead us to pinpoint a particular spot in this area. Maybe that small section in the Death Machine Letter that he asked to be printed in the newspaper.

This possibility is the reason I must include some other pieces of information in this book that may be relevant to this mystery. While you must make up your own mind on this, I would advise you not to disregard what you have just seen based on anything else you may disagree with.

It involves using the Zodiac 340 code as an overlay with the map as a grid to find marked locations. A map grid. This opens up hundreds of new possibilities. While I am one hundred percent positive that the 340 is used in this way, it seems to upset a lot of people at just the possibility of this idea. Some are dead set that this code, (which has been unsolved for decades upon decades) is a substitution cipher, only a substitution cipher, and nothing else!!! Any suggestion otherwise is just crazy. At least that is what I get a lot. I am confident that over time I will change opinions and open eyes as well as minds.

The thing which affects me the most about this view from some is that if they would consider what I am trying to show them, they maybe could actually find some sort of hidden order or transposition of the code that leads them to exactly what they are looking for. If there is a hidden substitution code in the 340, then it has something to do with the four quadrants and the dots that label them in the order of 0,1,2,3. Thousands of people, millions of dollars, and exponentially even more hours have been spent trying to solve the 340 just as it is. None have succeeded. This tells me that the 340 code is not a substitution code. It either has another use or it is just simply nothing.

I know that it is not just simply nothing, as I have found something it can actually be used for along with lots and lots of evidence and clues in the Zodiac letters to back it up. On my site, I list out every single one. In my first book, I list out the most important. In this book, I am just going to show a few.

That doesn't mean a substitution code or some other code could not be found based on what I am about to show you. I have a project that I have been working on that is based on this, but it is a huge amount of work. You can see this project on my site in the section titled "Transpositions of the 340 code". There as well as in my first book, I also show many other possible uses and ways messages could still be hidden in the 340 code. In fact, I believe there are. I think all three of these documents have more than one use. That is a common thing done in history with these types of codes. You can see a lot of it on my site. For a shill, I sure have wasted a lot of my life doing this and giving it away for free. Still, I do have to eat and live. This is a lot of work.

The next section will start by showing you a brief outline and comparison of the scale markers on the 340 code, the map, and the bomb drawing. I have to include something about it, or someone will say I am trying to hide it. I have had to include it in so many things that I have written that it starts just seeming like a waste of time and space repeating myself so much. Every single time I write something about the overlay, I have to start with the scale. So, this time I decided to put it all in a little bit of a different order. I would like to start chapter one with the map/bomb drawing overlay, as it is the whole point of the book and the most interesting part, but I have to remember that a lot of people who will be reading this may have never even heard of the Zodiac Killer. That is why I have to start with the basics of the case, which have been told and retold, written and rewritten thousands of times. The overlays are something completely new. No one dealt in the overlays until I came out with it. It makes me happy to see others trying new and different things.

Remember, no matter what, the overlay you have just seen is the one thing everyone should remember. So, let me show you a way to use the famous "unsolved" 340 code that no one had ever thought of. What you are about to see is what upsets people the most about my work. I believe it is just this one thing that makes so many try to blow me off completely.

If people listen to me about the map and bomb drawing, then they might listen to me about the 340 code being used as an overlay with the map as well. The hell of it is, I can show many clues Zodiac gave us that suggest this very thing. In fact, in some ways, I think the bomb drawing and map overlay may be a clue to all of this. I think he thought people would put those two things together relatively easily and figure out the 340 code is to be used in the same way. They may have figured it out relatively easily fifty years ago if the bomb drawing and map had printed in the papers as Zodiac requested. He may have also known they would not have printed the bomb drawing at that point and that someone would figure it out years down the line after it was too late to do anything about it. That could have been one of his tricks that he had gotten enjoyment from.

Whether the 340 is to be used in this fashion or not, I leave that up to you. Some will agree while others will not. Different views are a good thing, but we might as well use it in this way. It's not like it is being used for anything else. Besides, I am about to show you really good evidence and layout a short simple argument that just may convince you.

Chapter Five: The 340 Map Grid

Before we cut to the chase, it is at this point that I must show you the proof of scale. Each of these three documents has scale markers included on them. The map has one that was included when the map was printed, just as all maps do. The 340 code and the bomb schematic have scale markers that were produced when the SFPD photographed the documents for inclusion as evidence. (I once talked to a man who had acquired some of the letters from an auction. He gave me high definition scans or images of the letters he had made. Does it surprise you that some of these letters are in public hands? Serial Killer memorabilia is big money these days. You would think they would have kept all of the evidence for future use, like DNA and other things later down the line, just in case. The U.S. Marshall's office keeps cases of escaped convicts open for a mandatory one hundred years. Because you never know. I am not saying anything derogatory about this evidence being in public hands. It is just surprising because new technology may have gleaned new evidence from some of these letters at some point in time.)

Here is the scale marker on the Phillips 66 map. It states that one-inch equals approximately 6.4 miles. Or you could round it down to say one inch is more or less six miles.

Study it for a minute.

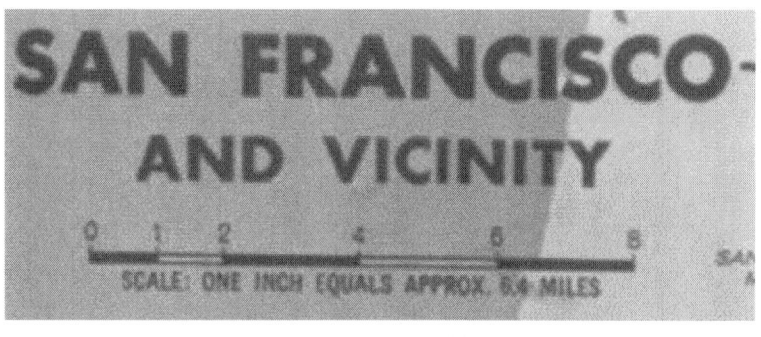

In an effort to avoid any confusion. What this means is that from the point marked 0 on the scale marker to the point marked 6 equals one inch.

This is the scale marker that was used by the San-Francisco Police Department when they photographed the images for evidence. This is the same scale marker used by police departments everywhere around the country.

It is exactly one inch. It is used so that it can provide the evidence in question with proof in relation to scale and size if it ever becomes relevant at a later point in time. This is done with all photographs that are taken into evidence. For example, bullets, shoe prints, guns, or anything where some context of scale needs to be provided to give investigators or anyone viewing the photographs and idea of the actual size of what is in the image in question.

Here is a comparison I made with the SFPD scale marker in relation to the scale marker provided on the Phillips 66 map.

When I posted my first models, one could have simply put a piece of paper on the screen and made two marks on the paper to represent the one inch the SFPD scale marker provided. Then it could be placed over the scale marker on the map to see if the two marks were consistent with the 0 and 6. A simple way of checking the scale on both documents.

I have had some say to me, "That only provides us scale in one direction and not both."

Well, it provides a scale for the entire thing, and one could tell if the image looks distorted. You can match these documents to scale with each other using a computer or a simple app on a phone these days. When matching the sizes, the entire image will get larger or smaller. Not just one way. This is called the aspect ratio. That is the exact same way police investigators and professionals do it all around the world. All I can do is try to explain it to someone who has no experience with such things and hope they get it.

Before I go on, I want to make sure I explain the aspect ratio very clearly. For example, when an image is resized, either larger or smaller, the size changes horizontally in the exact same aspect ratio is it does vertically. Every image editing software that is known does this unless you change it. I will give you an example.

This is Microsoft Paint. The most simple image editing software known to man. When you choose to resize an image, it is already set to keep the aspect ratio the same.

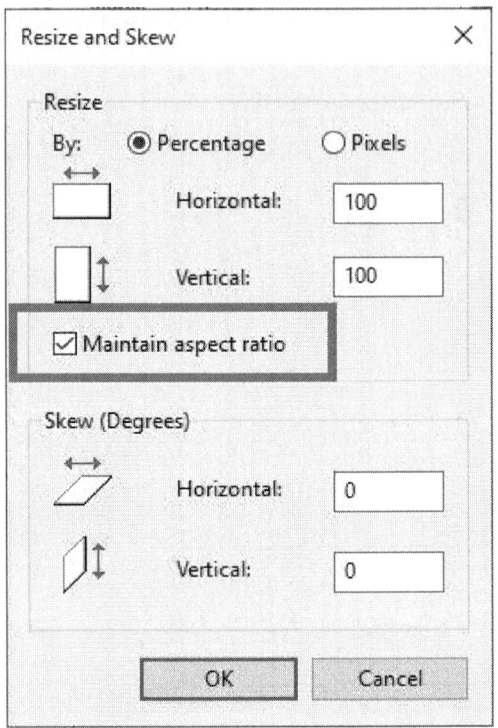

The print outs that I first used when I discovered this was already matched to one another's scale. It was a complete accident. Almost like fate. Later, I used software that was a little more advanced so that I could compare the two images to one another in order to create digital scale models for animations and other things. Also, to make models so that anyone could print them out without having to do all of the work themselves, but I invite anyone to test it for themselves. In fact, I want you to.

The fact is, that if the image had been altered to try to change the scale to make it fit, it would be painfully obvious as the image would be distorted. Anyone, even a child would be able to tell. Here is an example of what I mean. This image has had the aspect ratio changed on it by a factor of ten horizontally while left alone vertically in Microsoft Paint. A very, very small change, but it is very obvious as the image is distorted.

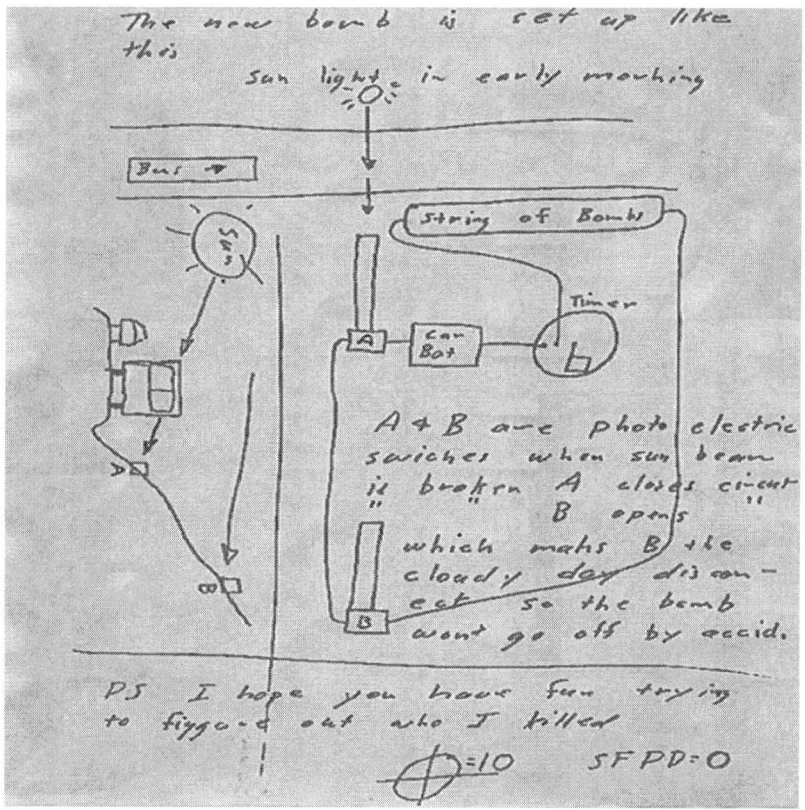

The more you change it, the more obvious it would be.

Here is the same image that has been changed by a factor of 30 horizontally. Still, not a lot but it is very obvious.

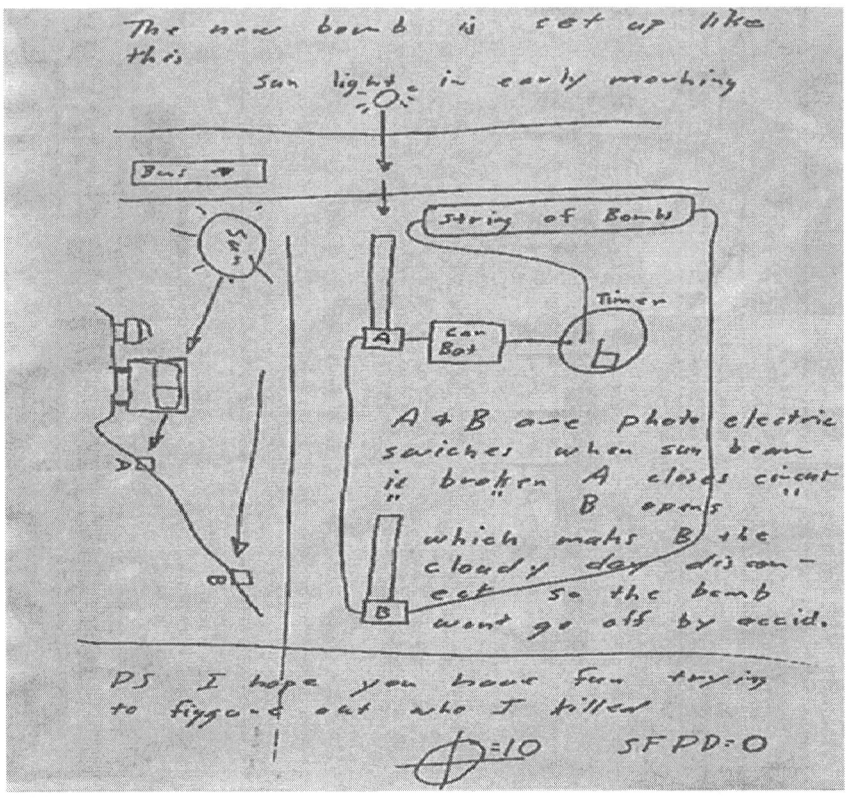

Do you see what I mean? This argument might effective for people who have had no experience with such things and sway them into thinking it was some kind of trick, but these days almost everyone does. The fact is that even if the aspect ratio was off by a little, that it would not matter as even if it is close you will get the same results. That is why I invite anyone to try it for themselves. Don't believe me, try it for yourself. A smart person doesn't take anything at face value anyway. A wise person would want to know more, but blindly trying to come up with excuses why it should not be believed it just the work of those who have their own motivations for wanting it to be dismissed. Still, I don't know why. They could use this information to further their own work. It makes no sense. At least offer proof of why the scale is wrong. It amazed me how many people were willing to dismiss this based on the comments of a few people who offered no proof of why it wouldn't work. It is so easy to test and anyone with a cell phone can do it. So, I invite everyone to test it. And I hope the people who can actually use it.

I made digital models and animations of these overlays to offer better examples and to show the scale compared side by side at the beginning of each animation so I could show that there is no trickery behind this. While I could put the animations in an eBook, this book is also meant to be in print. All I can offer are still images. You can find animations of the overlays on my site.

I apologize for even having to go into all of this, but I have learned from experience that it will only cause problems later down the line if I don't. I did the best I could with what I had, which I didn't have much to work with. Still, I think I did a pretty damn good job.

Here I will show you a comparison of the bomb drawing and the map on the actual documents in relation to one another. Look at the lower left hand of the image.

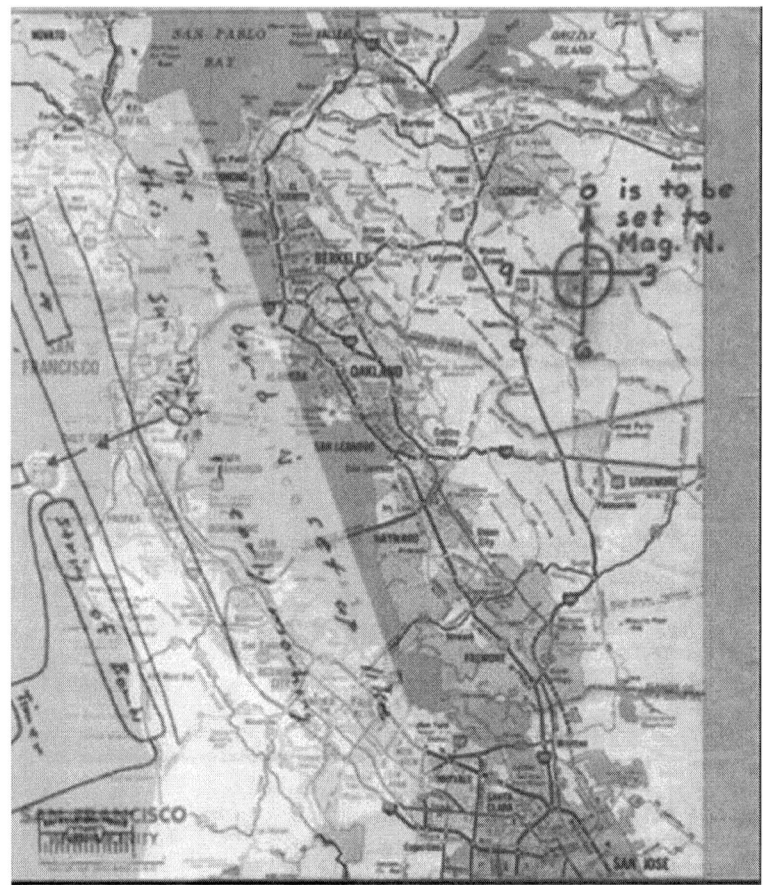

The image above was the beginning of the animation I created that started by showing the scale on both documents was the same. The bomb drawing would then move across the map to show the final overlay, which you have already seen. Next, we get to move on to how the 340 code plays into all of this.

At the bottom of the image of the 340 code that I supplied earlier, you will see another scale marker that was provided by the SFPD when they took photographs of the evidence. The marker is exactly 3 inches long.

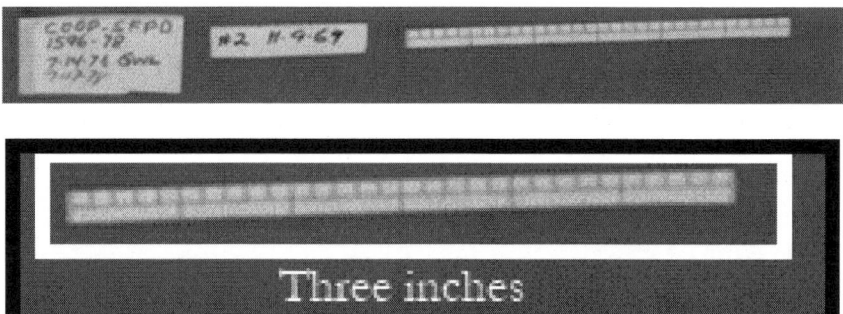

Three inches

Here you will see the scale markers of all three documents in relation to one another.

These markers are all you need to scale these documents. In a perfect world, we would try this on the originals, but I am not even sure where they are or who has them. Still, if I am right, Zodiac meant for these to be printed in the newspaper and solved by regular people. Just like his famous 408 code was printed in a paper and solved. If they had been, this may have been discovered long ago and if prints in a newspaper can be used then I have no problem working with high definition color images and scans of the original documents that have proof of scale already provided. Do you remember this image of the 340 from earlier? Notice the pair of dice.

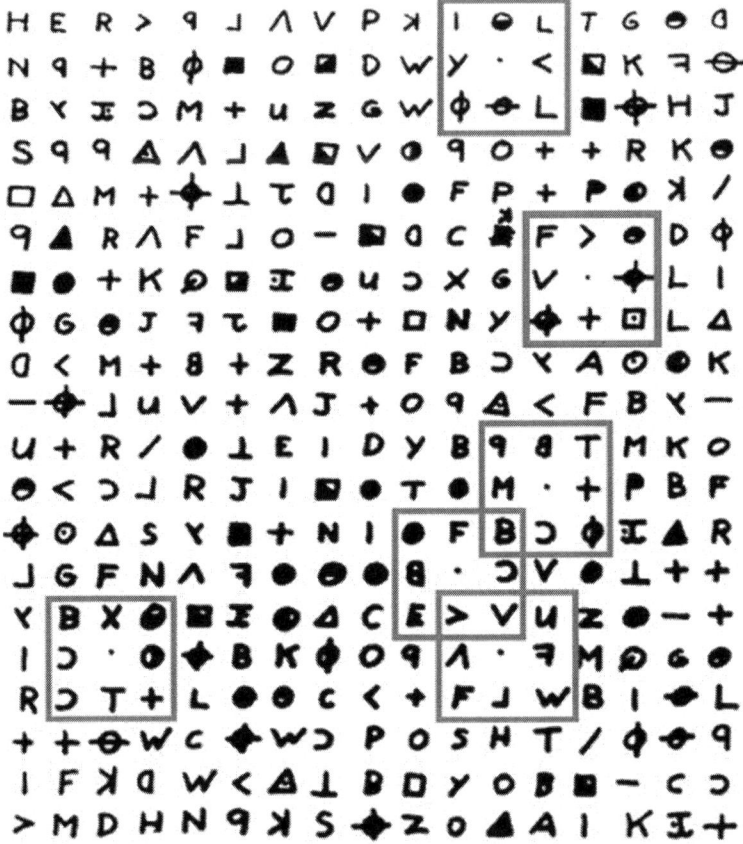

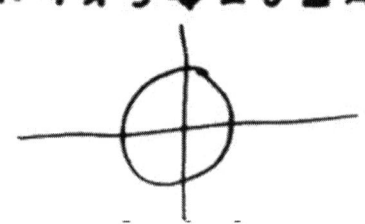

These dots that number the four quadrants of the code are key to what I am about to show you. First, I am going to give you a brief overview of the main clues that lead me to use the 340 as a grid overlay on the map to find marked locations. While I believe this is the primary function of the 340, it is important to remember I also believe it contains many more uses and secrets. In my first book, I show many different possibilities based on systems that have been used quite frequently throughout history.

Though I can not include them here because this is meant to be a much shorter and much more affordable version of my work, I do want to make clear that this is not the only function of this code and that I have works out there that will show you much, much more than what you are about to see.

One of the first clues to what I am about to show you came from the Zodiac Killer Halloween card that was mailed to Journalist Paul Avery of the San Francisco Chronicle. It had this strange symbol etched into it.

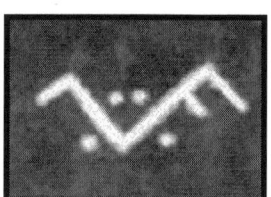

Here is a restored and colorized image of the Halloween card that I created from a black and white scan of the original card. This card is a mystery as no one seems to know exactly where it came from or what company created it. I restored this image to give a more accurate example of the card in color as the image that most people know is a fake from the movie Zodiac. Why does this matter? Since we have discovered the use of overlays in the codes and letters and size and aspect ratio play into this, it is very important. The card from the movie was created by a very talented artist, but they blew up the size of the original card, changed the aspect ratio, and cropped off part of the card. You can see on my site the differences between the two and just how much different they actually are. This is important because the eyes on the Halloween Card could be some kind of an overlay key themselves. Notice how they stand out.

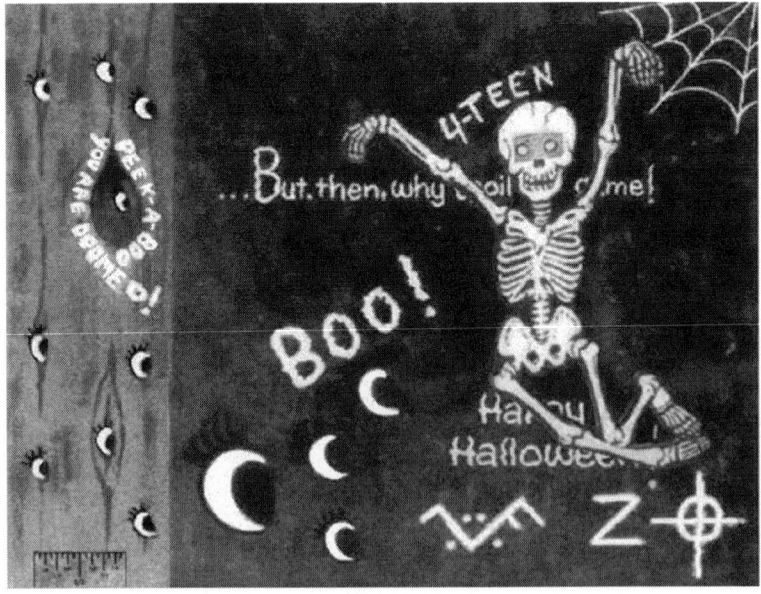

They also follow the theme of thirteen and holes stamped out in some of the other cards. I recognized this symbol on the bottom of the card as a Masonic Square and Compass. Compass…. Like the compass, Zodiac had drawn onto the Philipps 66 map that was used in the alignment for the bomb drawing overlay.

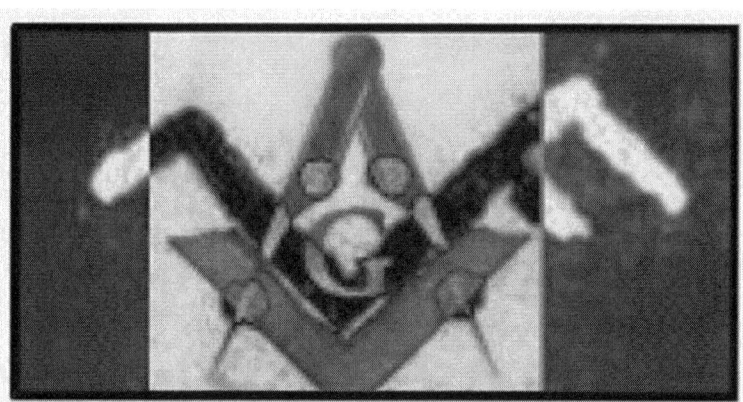

Zodiac also made many references to "Par-a-dice" in his letters. He spelled it exactly in that manner. Pair-o-dice. This was when I started noticing all of the clues that made some kind of reference to dots. That was when I saw the dots on the 340 code as something more than just numbering the four quadrants. I saw them as dice. So I drew pens around them, like in the pigpen cipher we talked about earlier in reference to the pen card that the 340 code came with.

Then I started noticing all of the clues on the Halloween card. I can connect everything written on the Halloween card to the 340 code. EVERYTHING!!!!

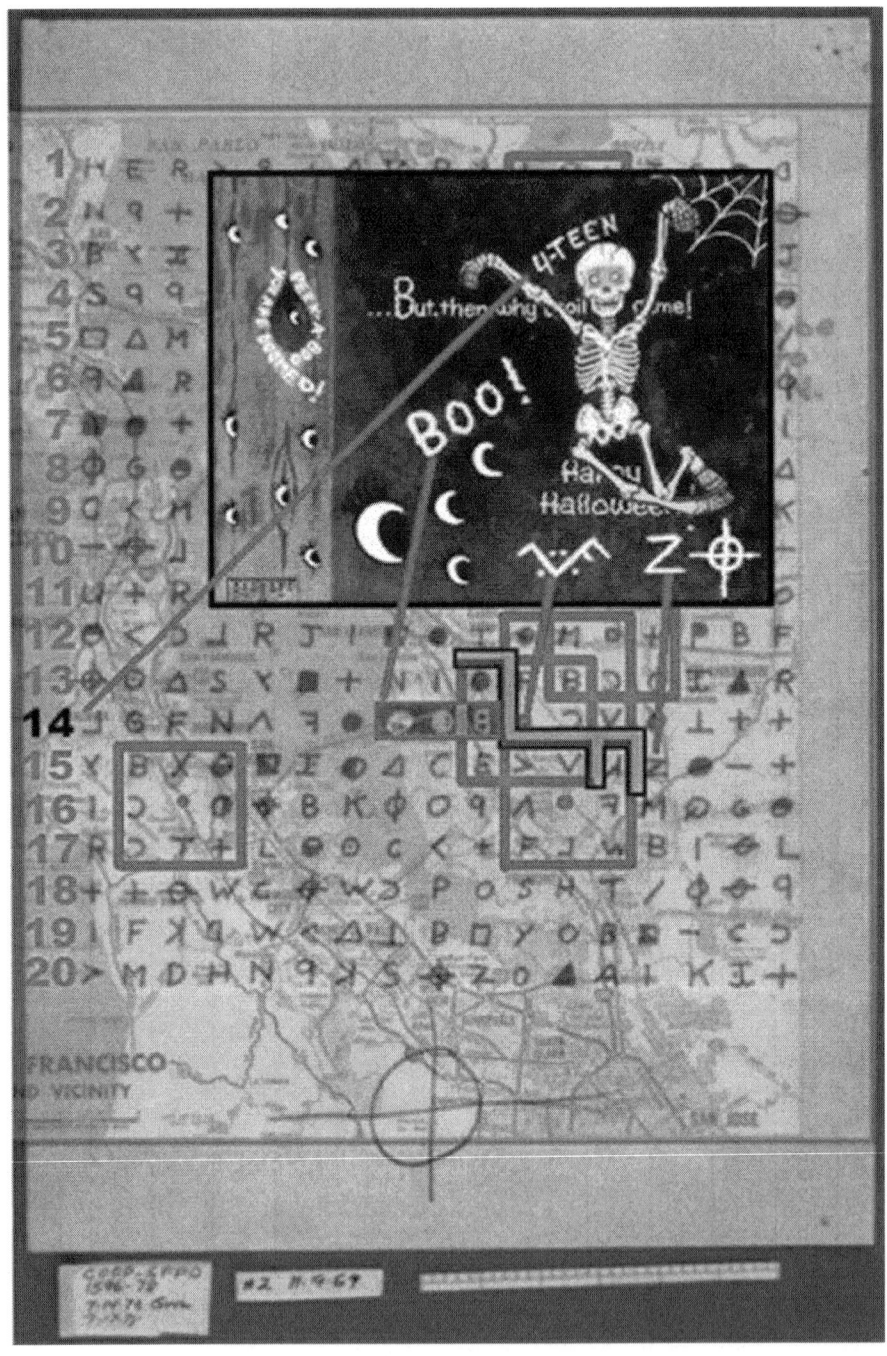

They say an image is worth a thousand words but I guess I should still supply some explanation of what is going on here. On the card, you see the words, "Fourteen", "Boo", and the square and compass that is followed by the letter 'Z".

On the 14th line of the 340, you will see the word "Boo". After you draw the pens onto the code, you will see the rest of that strange symbol on the card embedded into the dice followed by the letter 'Z". He is telling us there are some important clues to the 340 on the card. The biggest one is the Square and Compass hidden in the strange symbol. Notice the symbol also has dots just like the 340 code. Things that appear no to belong.

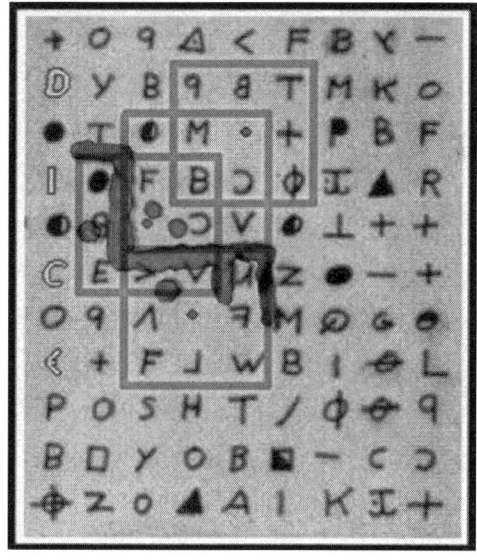

Notice the word "dice" hidden in the code right beside the cluster of dice or pens that the strange symbol is embedded into. It is also an exact match. What are the odds of that? Also, remember the puzzle from the Exorcist letter that you saw earlier.

This is when I started thinking about the bomb overlay and the compass that he had hand-drawn onto the map. I started looking at the squares I had drawn around the dots on the 340 code. Then I thought, "The square and compass are overlaid onto one another. What if a square on the 340 is meant to overlay onto the compass on the map?"

I know what you are thinking, "Yeah, but how do you know which square to align with the compass?" I thought the very same thing. So, I started studying the pens on the code and that is when I saw it. Zodiac left a marker inside the pen we were supposed to use.

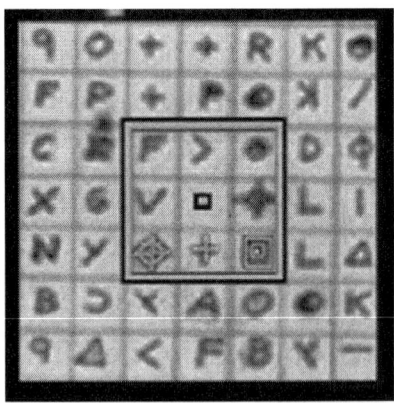

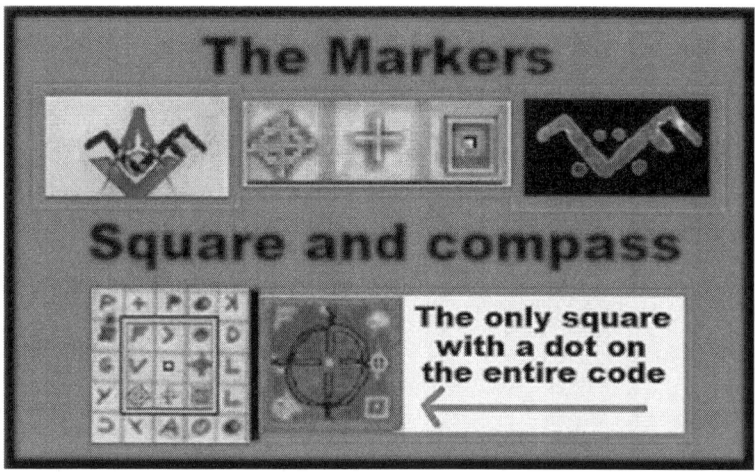

This also happens to be the same section of the code that was Zodiac pointed out in the Exorcist letter puzzle.

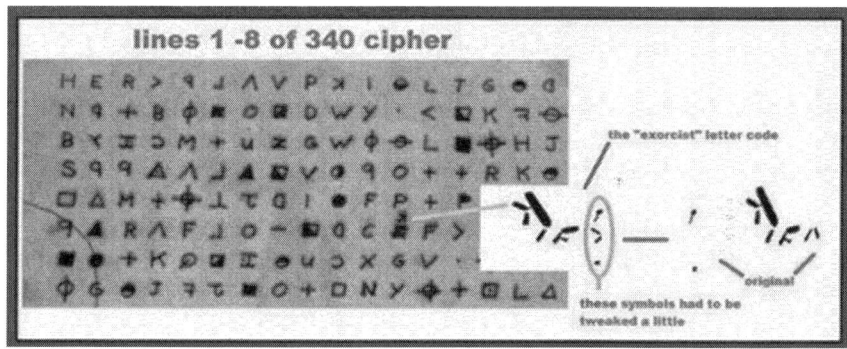

Remember, the puzzle that was an exact match when it was overlaid onto the envelope it came with.

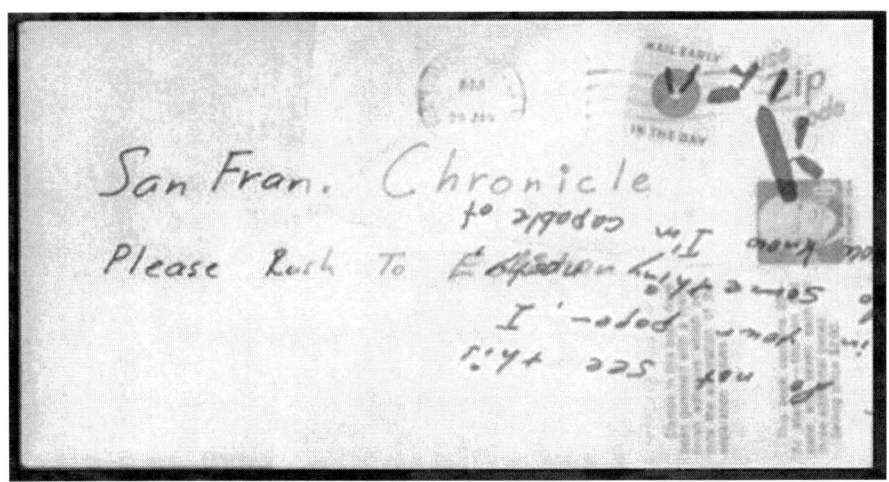

This was when all of the pieces started falling into place for me. Now, even you have to admit, this is a hell of a lot of coincidence. That is a hell of a lot of evidence for overlays. Nothing can have that much coincidence. You could have won the lottery ten times over before this much coincidence.

So, now I have found all of these clues leading us to overlay the 340 code onto the map. That just scratches the surface. I found a lot more, but I am trying to keep it as simple and straight forward as I can while showing the most important and impressive things. You have to admit, if you have made it to this point, I am starting to win you over. I found a hell of a lot more.

There are more things on the Halloween card that connect directly to the 340 code as well. You can find them on my site, but since you have read this far, I have a present for you. From me to you. At the end of this book, I am going to place a link. If you follow it or type it into your address bar on your web browser then it will lead you to a place where you can download a PDF of my first book for free. All that matters are that people read it and see it. I encourage you to share it with your friends.

We are not finished yet, but we are almost there. You have yet to see the best parts. In one of his letters, Zodiac stated the map code involved radians. No one knew how to find these radians. I found how to find them. While I have figured out part of the code, I have not nearly figured out all of it. So, I need your help to either solve the rest or to find someone who might be able to. I know they are out there; they just have not seen how far I have come. I know it probably involves navigation skills and a little trigonometry. Besides the marked locations you can find, there is a way to use the clues, the overlays, the radians, to find one specific place. It is my hope that someone out there takes this seriously and doesn't think it is just some crazy Zodiac Killer theory. I hope they can use this to figure out the rest and find whatever it is Zodiac was leading us to. The next part requires skills I myself do not possess. Only someone with a lifetime of experience can see the clues and know exactly what it is they are hinting to. Now, I can show you the rest. Here is the 340 code/map overlay.

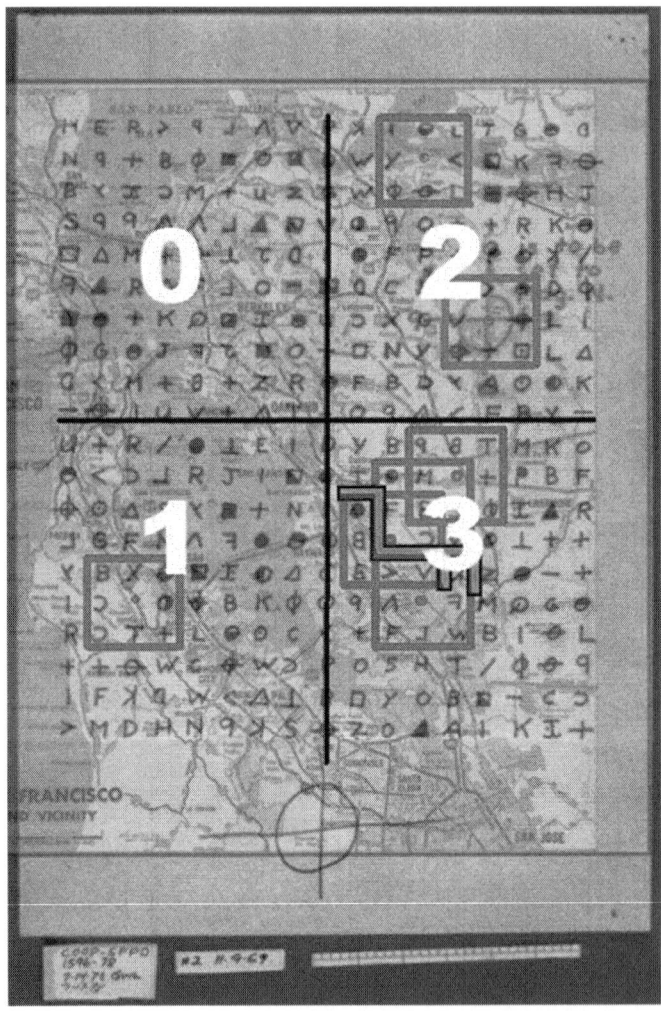

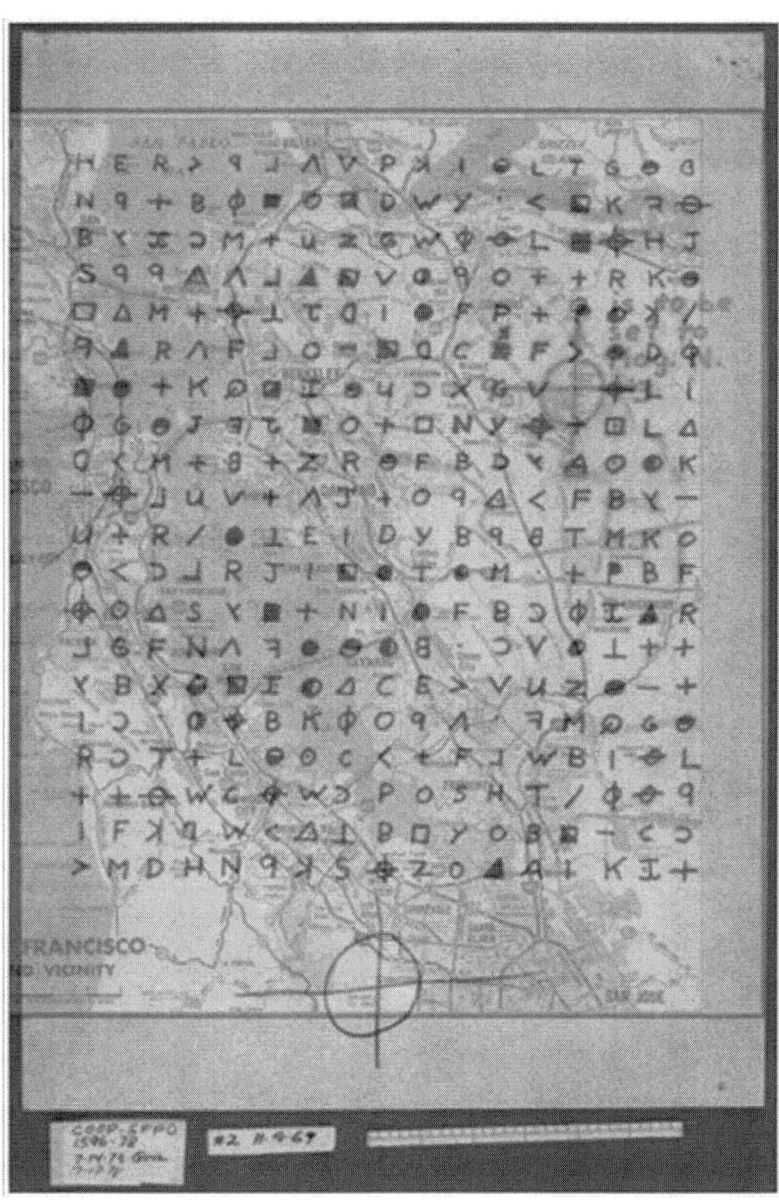

Zodiac had to use a grid overlay just to create the 340 code.

I supplied a clean version as well, but remember that I have a hell of a lot more information on this if you want to see it all.

Zodiac stated that the map code involved radians.

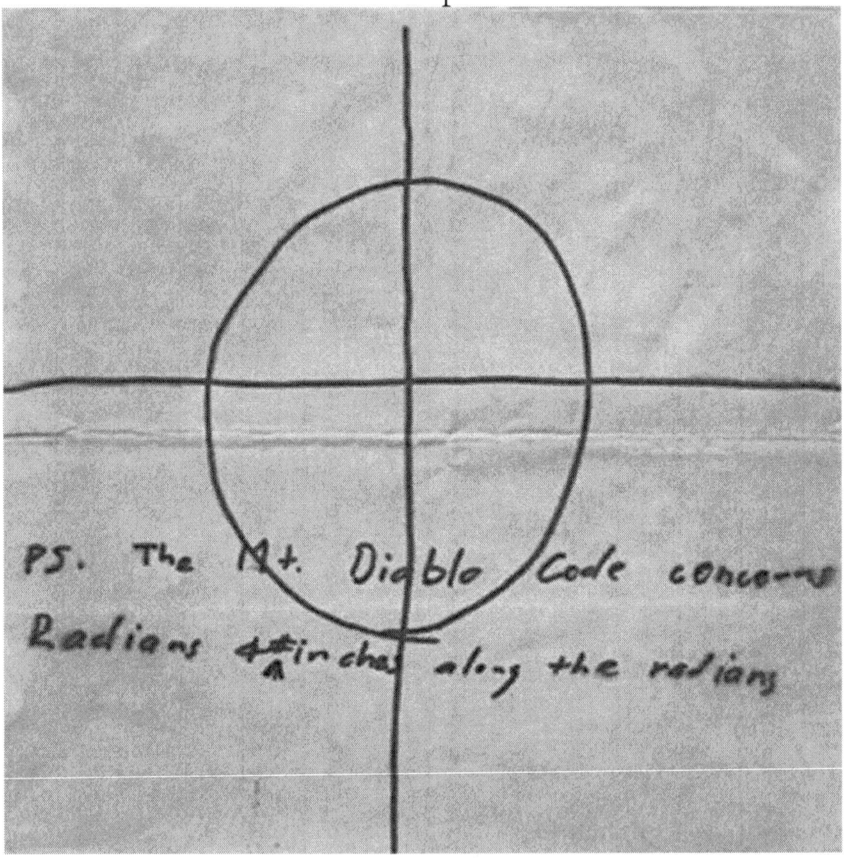

P.S. The Mt. Diablo Code concerns Radians + # inches along the radians

Seeing this clue led me to discover a few more that

Zodiac had left in his letters that looked just like this one.

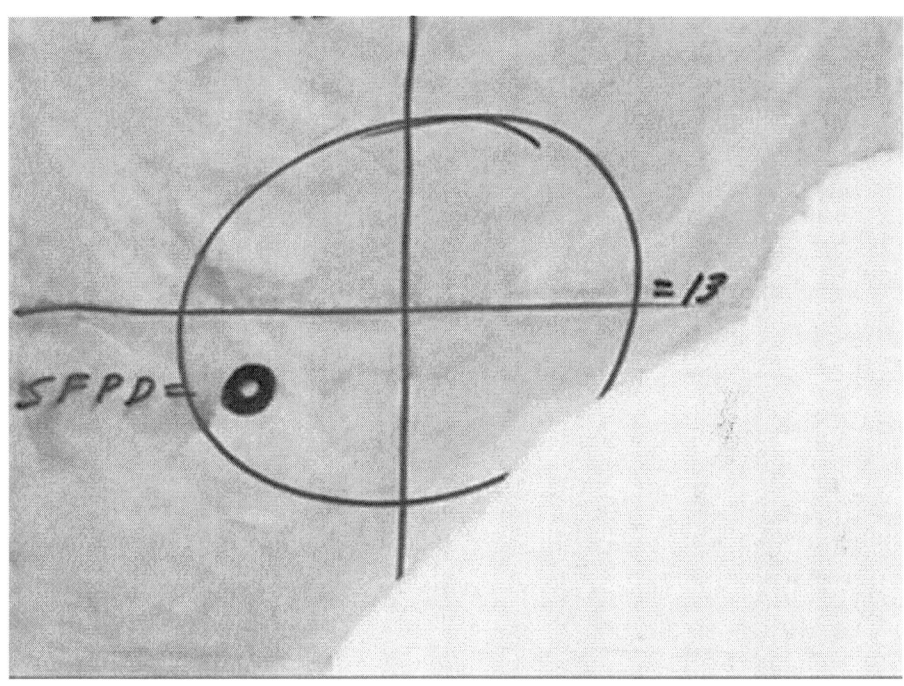

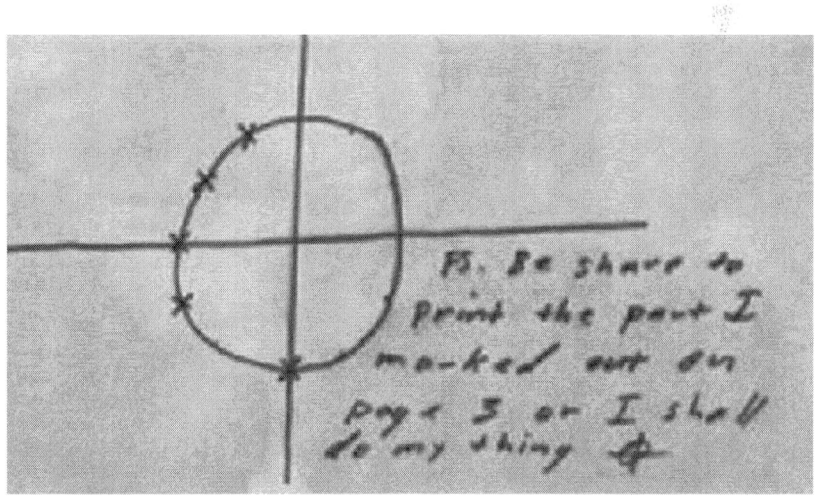

All three of these sections are very important and they give us even more special insights into the 340 code. At this point, you must be starting to realize all of the clues Zodiac gave us about overlaying and the multitude of clues that concern the 340 code.

Before I show you what these three clues mean, I have to familiarize you with what exactly what a radian is. Radians are found by using circles and angles. They are used in things like navigation and sighting in the scopes on guns just to give you a couple of practical examples. The reason no one could figure out how to find these radians is one reason no one could ever figure out how to use the map. Most thought that like the 340 code, the map must all be a trick as well. They thought it was just nothing but something designed to keep people busy trying to solve nothing. The map and 340 are actually something real and they have more in common than everyone just thinking they were some kind of trick designed to keep everyone busy trying to solve nothing. In fact, they are very connected. The 340/map grid is the tool used to find the radians on the map.

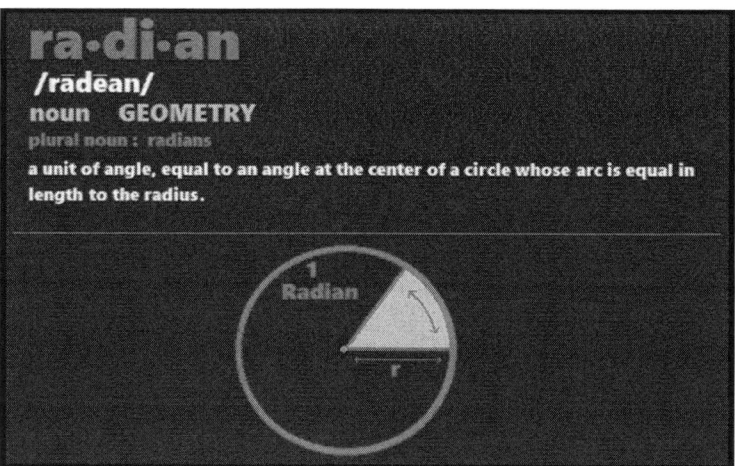

Below is a diagram of the scope of a rifle and how Mrads are used to sight the gun in. MRAD is just short for milli-radian. It is like the difference between a meter and a millimeter. This might give you a better idea of how radians are meant to work. You can look up how to use radians in a trigonometry book. They are usually used in relation to navigation. Given the military connections to Zodiac and the fact that the radians we are using involve a map, then it is a safe bet it has something to do with navigation or numbering the map like a grid to find locations.

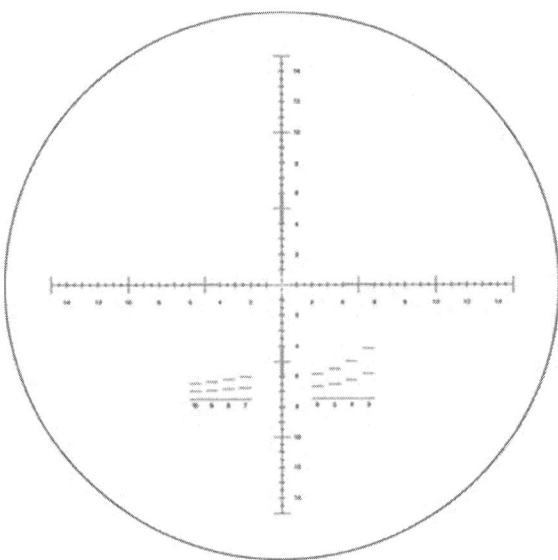

Now I am going to show you how to use the 340 to find the radians and how the three clues you saw before prove that I am right. It is all about the four quadrants on the 340 and the dots. Here it is, step by step.

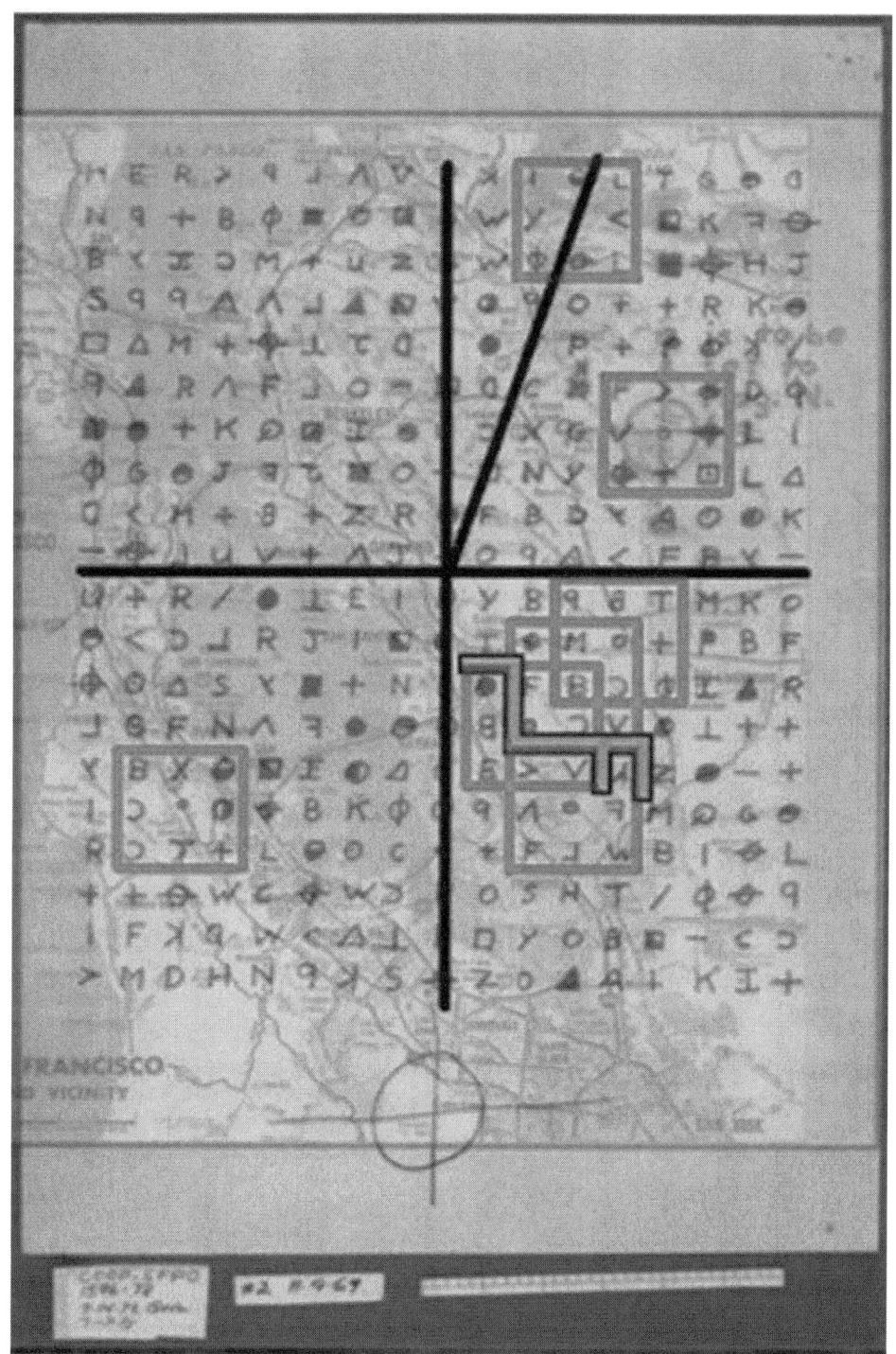

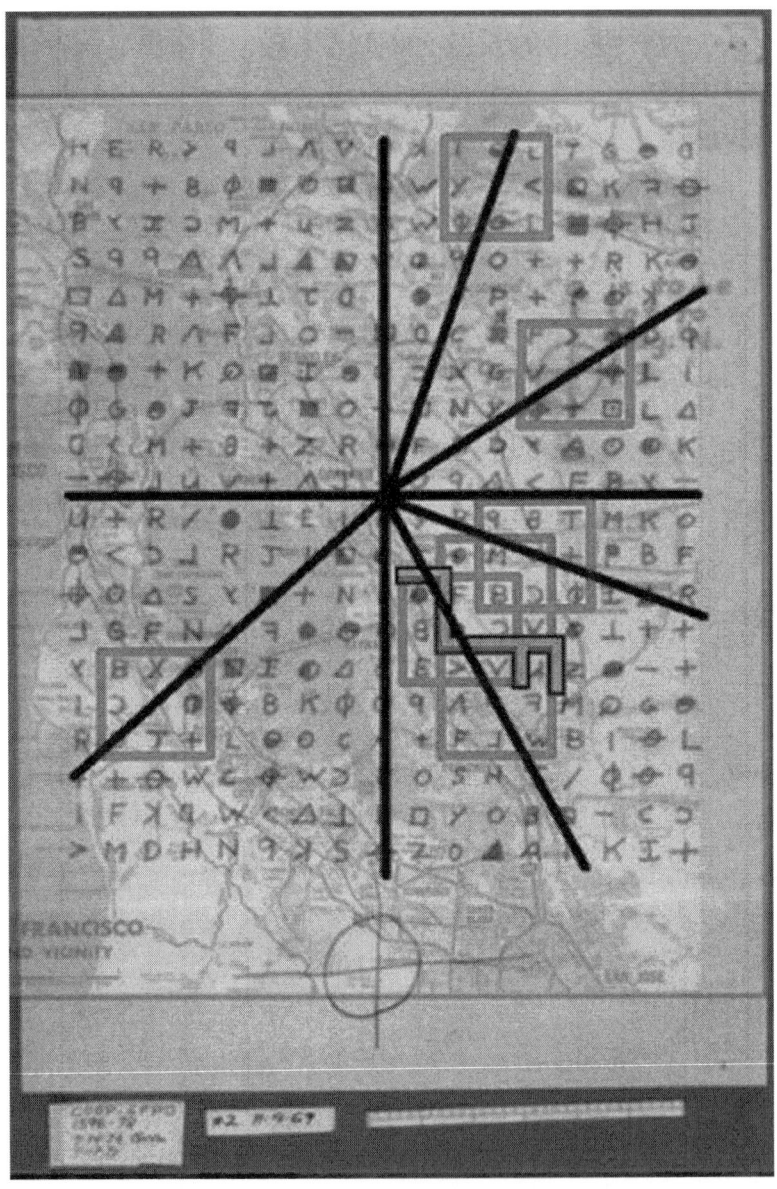

You just start drawing lines from the point of origin like on every grid you ever worked in math class to the dots on the 340.

How do I know this is what you are supposed to do? These clues. First, let's look at this clue.

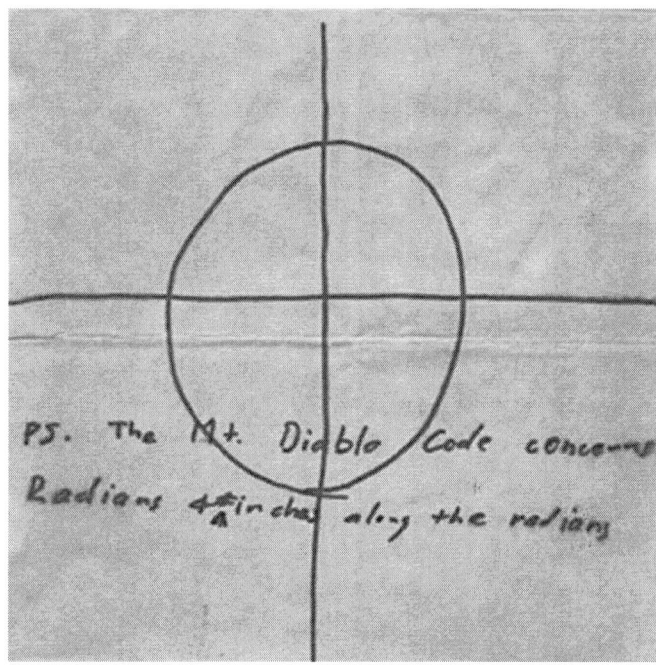

The Zodiac crossed circle was a clue to it all along. This clue also tells us to label the inches along the radians. I can label the inches but the rest is up to someone else. Now, let's look at the next clue.

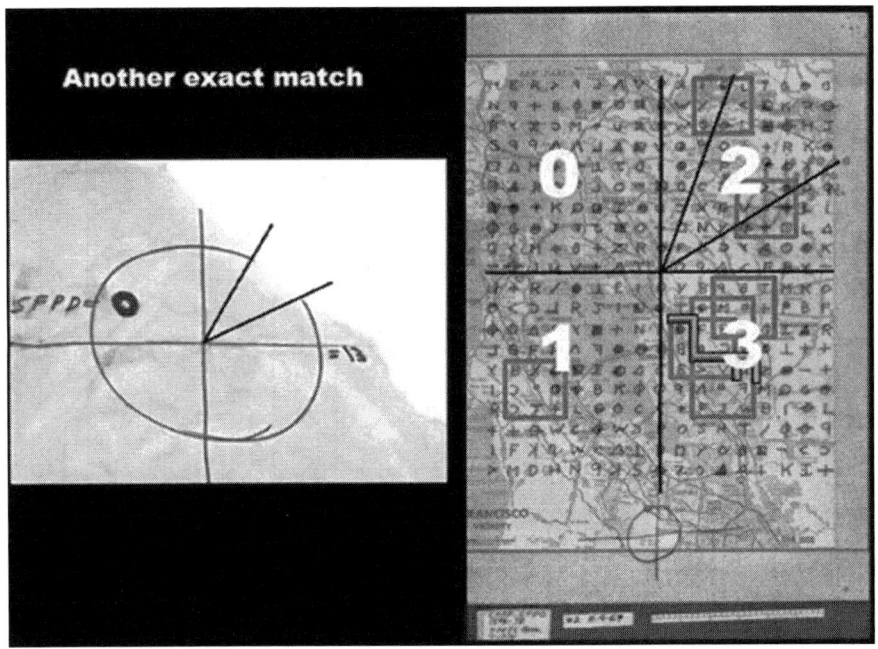

It matches the 340 exactly when mirrored. A zero in the upper left-hand quadrant, two points in the upper right-hand quadrant and the two lower quadrants equal 13. This was a clue to the dots on the 340 all along. How many clues have I shown you to the 340 and all of this? I lost count a long time ago. It also suggests mirroring may play a part somewhere in the puzzle. That is something I have been thinking about recently. I wish I could go into it more with you.

Now, let's look at the final and most important clue. The clue that shows incontrovertible evidence that this is the right way to use the 340 and map together and that the dots are meant to be used not only to mark locations but to find the long looked for and thought to be nonexistent radians.

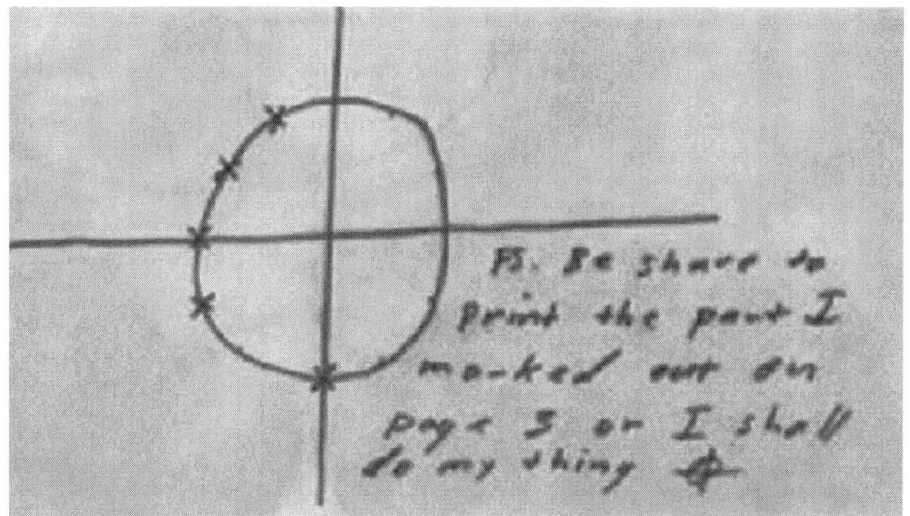

Look closely as this crossed circle. Notice here that we have more dots, following a theme of clues. I am guessing that in relation to the message scrawled beside this clue that the message he stated was to be printed in the paper plays some kind of role in all of this. I have everything you need in my first book.

Why did he put dots on one part of this circle and x's on the other? Notice that this resembles a clock. Timekeeping, which is what the Zodiac was originally used for. It is also used for navigation and finding specific places. Now, I am going to draw lines from the point of origin on this drawing to the dots that line the outer circle of the Zodiac cross, just like we just did on the 340. Let's see what it looks like.

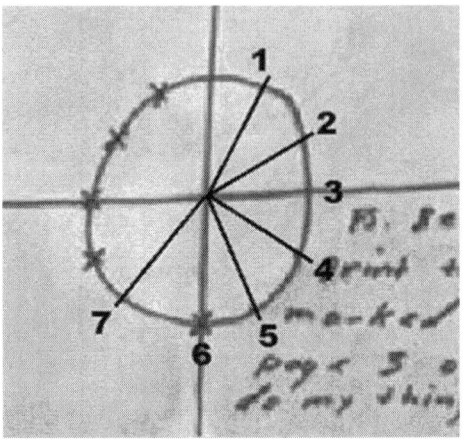

Now, let's compare this to the 340.

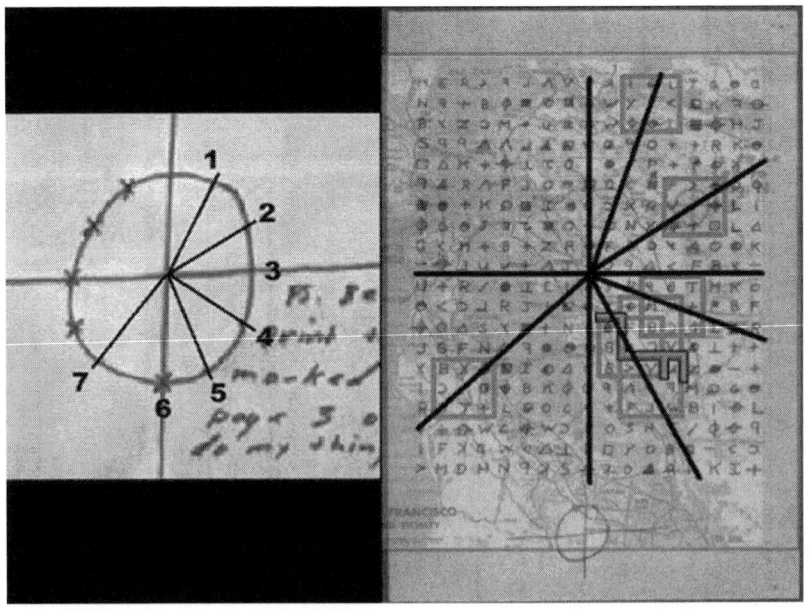

How many times have I said this so far? Another exact match and what are the odds of that. You could have won the lottery twenty times over by now before all of this, everything I have shown you in this book could be a coincidence. No way in hell. Everything you have seen is by design.

Well, there it is. The most important things I have found, learned, and figured out about the Zodiac killer codes. When I tried to tell the world, no one gave a shit. Just the opposite, the establishment was not only completely silent, but they also hoped I would disappear. Who knows, they may get their wish in the end. I just wish they would take it seriously and use it, but there is another way. I can try my best to show the world. Then who knows. Someone may actually figure out the parts I am missing.

So, it is my mission to show this to the world. I put it all on a blog for free, but the reality of the world we live in is that no one will take you seriously if you put it on the internet and give it away for free. That is just a sad fact of life son and one that someone had warned me about. On the flip side, if you do it the way that everyone will take it seriously, people will call you a sell-out and say you just did it for money. Eating, paying the electric bill, and having a place to live would be nice. There is nothing wrong with making money from your hard work as every other single person on earth does.

To be taken seriously, and to have people listen, you have to do things like write an actual book (like I have done) and get people to read it. Anyone who has ever been through this knows exactly what I am talking about. When you are new to the game, you learn the hard way. No matter what you do, people are going to attack you. So forget them. The good news is that even more people will get it and love it.

I don't have money to buy ads and things. I don't have anyone who is going to help me. Everything you have seen and everything that has brought me this far, I have done myself. While you are reading this, I am out there somewhere posting links and trying to get people to either read a book, look at a site, or read an article in the hopes it will spark their curiosity enough to want to learn more. While you are reading this, people who can't see past it are either attacking me, telling me to go away, or calling me a shill. I'm fine with that. Nothing worth doing is ever easy and I'll be damned if I will lay down so someone else can come out years from now and claim they did this. It has happened to me before and I have put way too much work into this. This book is not just about the Zodiac codes. In a lot of ways, it is about my own personal journey through all of this. The best way I can explain it is to include my experiences along with it. You never know, I could die tomorrow, but at least I did something while I was here.

This is not the only thing I have done. I have gotten into writing fiction and other stories. Things that are less of a headache and actually a lot easier to get published. I had an actual publisher interested at one point, but I got sick and was not able to do anything for a long time. I was not ready with the final version. Life goes on and maybe at some point, I can do it again. As far as all of this goes, all that is important is that people know about it.

I am going to include just a few more images that you might find interesting. They may be useful, but to be honest, I just like them.

The radians labeled in inches.

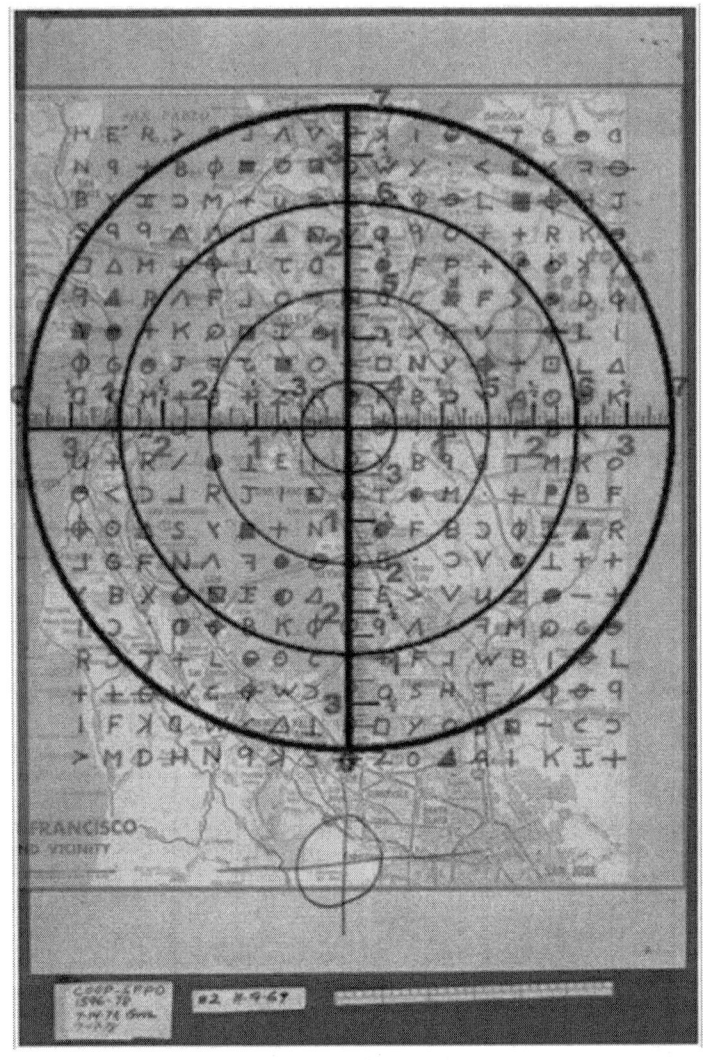

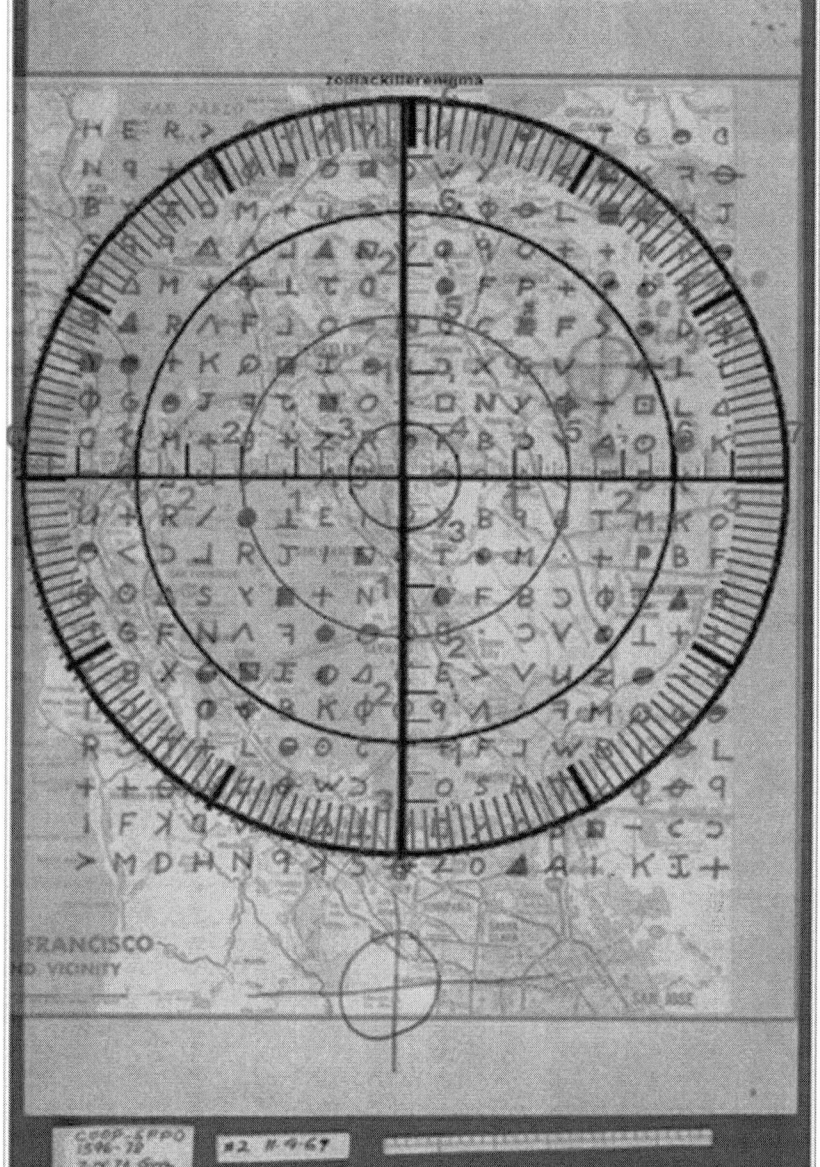

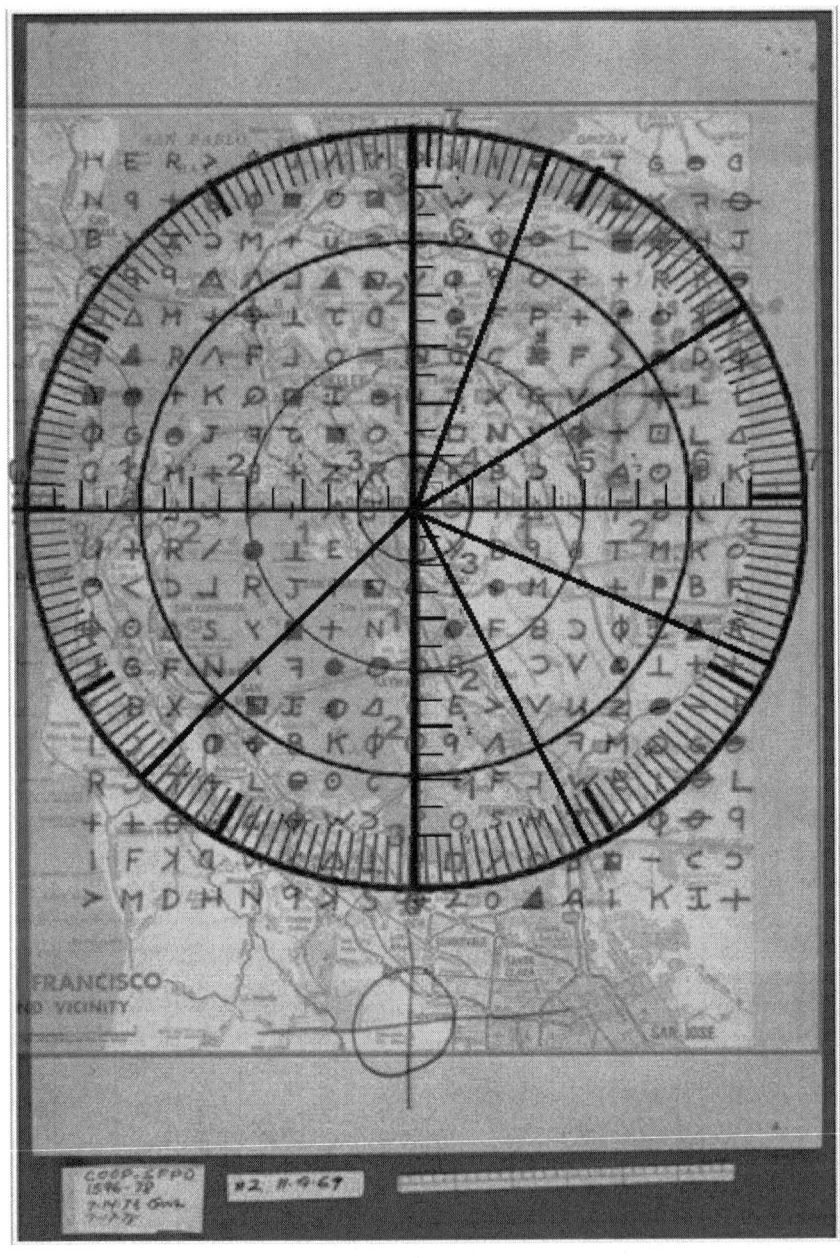

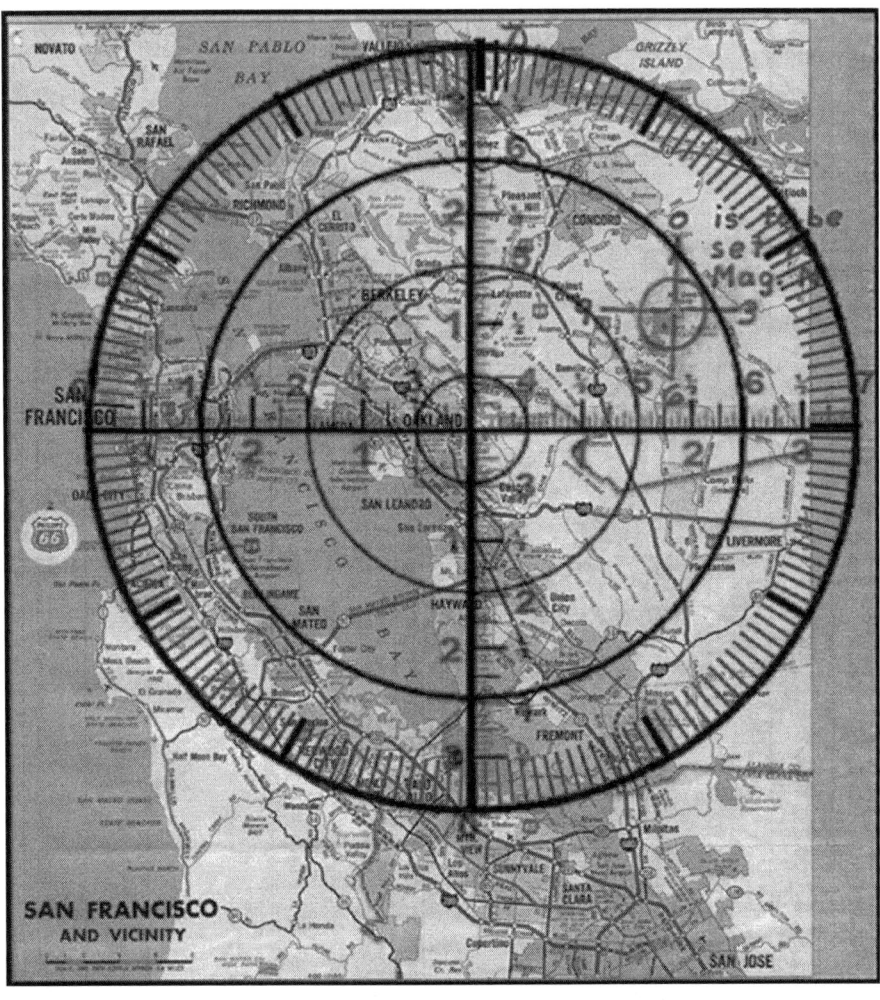

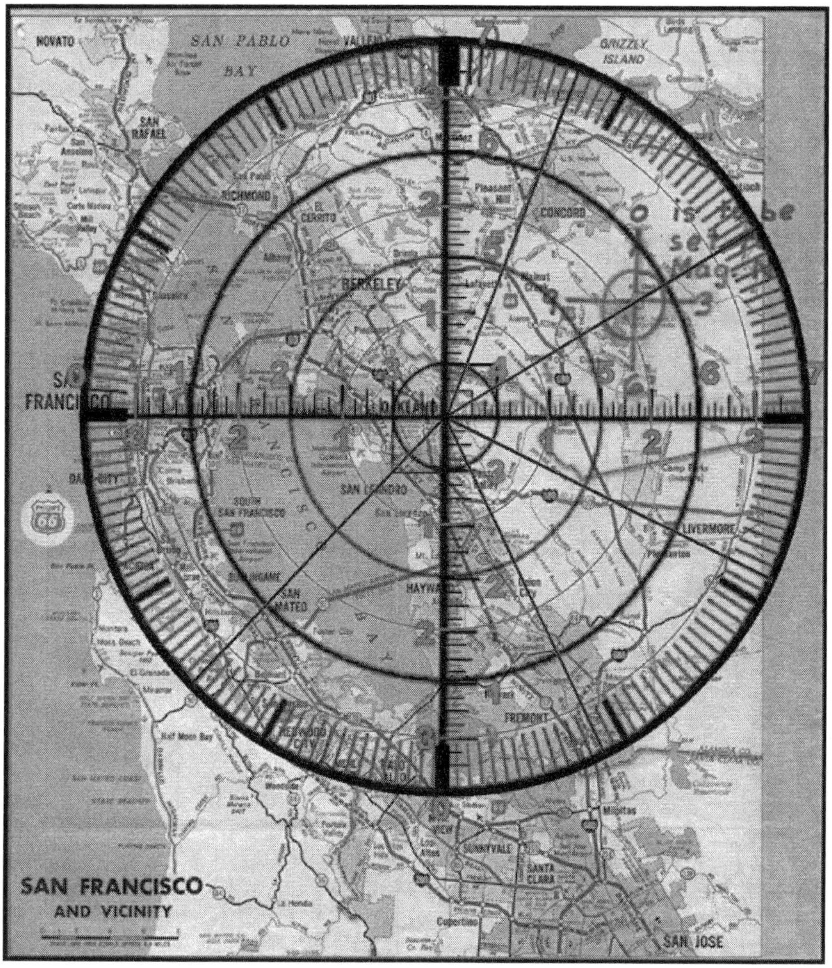
SAN FRANCISCO
AND VICINITY
SAN PABLO
BAY
NOVATO
GRIZZLY
ISLAND
SAN RAFAEL
RICHMOND
EL CERRITO
CONCORD
BERKELEY
OAKLAND
SAN LEANDRO
SOUTH SAN FRANCISCO
BURLINGAME
SAN MATEO
HAYWARD
LIVERMORE
FREMONT
Half Moon Bay
SUNNYVALE
SANTA CLARA
Cupertino
SAN JOSE
Milpitas
FRANCISCO

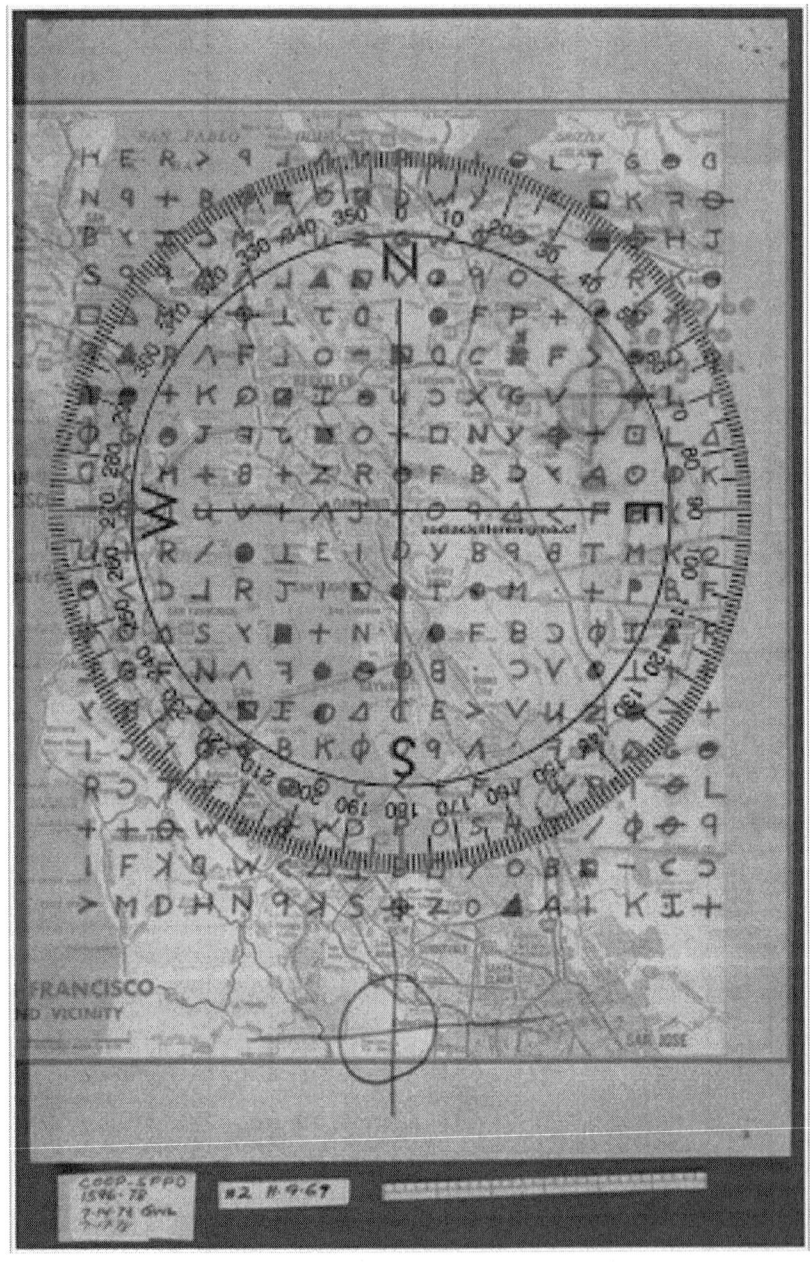

ABOUT THE AUTHOR

R. S. Clemons was born in a small town in the Appalachian Mountains of Eastern Kentucky. The son of an attorney and an author, he went to a little school called Caney Elementary when he was a child where he learned some of the things that helped him with solving this puzzle. There is more about him than could ever put into this small section. He likes to say that he just an average guy and that there is nothing really special about him. He is a very humble, kind, and courteous person. He has had some interesting life experiences and could tell you some really good stories. R.S. has not had a boring and sheltered life. At least up until now. It is said that he has calmed down from the wilder days of his youth. He said once, "I have been some places, seen some things, you know the rest of the song." R.S. often likes to remind peoples that all you have in life are your experiences. So, make the most of your time and don't commit the sin of turning your back on it. You only get one ticket on this ride. When you are lying on your death bed, you will realize that if you don't already. Time is the most valuable thing you have. Don't spend it on things and people that are not worth it. Don't be afraid to take risks. You never know when they might pay off. He says that he regrets the things he didn't do, the chances that he didn't take, more than the things he did. Even when they landed him in trouble, they made him who he is and brought him to where he is at. That is one of the biggest reasons why he wrote this book. Knowing the kind of attention, it would draw to him, he said he didn't want to regret not doing it and not sharing what he found with the world. He didn't want to wonder what would have happened if he only had instead of not sharing it. He plans to do more books on this subject in the future as well as to branch out into other areas and genres. As promised, here is a link that will allow you to download his first book for free. Please, share it with your friends. It has way more in it than this book does. He really hopes this helps someone to take the steps that he could not. Here is

the link to download my first book for free parts 1 and 2
https://drive.google.com/file/d/1e6EVVCVUvHKoCisXEtN7jWHQ7uVbG
dyf/view?usp=sharing

https://drive.google.com/file/d/1GhlAfgJqbvpmsvyznHZGRyR-
u5le519r/view?usp=sharing

   If this is the eBook version then you can just click on the link. If this is
a print version you will have to type the link into your address bar. Here
are some other sites with good people you may want to check out.

Richard Grinell -   www.zodiacciphers.com

Michael Morford a.k.a. Mort – www.zodiackillersite.com

Marcello Leandro – www.blogspot.zodiackillertheory.com

Me – www.blogspot.zodiackillerenigma.com

David Oranchack -   www.oranchak.com

David's site has some really helpful tools and things for code breakers as
does Richard's and as does mine. These are the only sites that you will
find these tools.

Let's not forget the two main people who made it all possible for
everyone to access all of the Zodiac Material. They were the first and
deserve credit.

www.zodiackiller.com

www.zodiackillerfacts.com

All of these guys get little to nothing for their efforts. Don't forget that.

U.S.A.

Printed in Great Britain
by Amazon

44147590R00079

The Zodiac Killer Map

Black & White Edition

R.S. Clemons

ATTENTION

This book was meant to be printed in color with color images.
This edition has been formatted to be in black and white with
black and white images to make it more affordable for those who
wish to own a copy for their collection but at a reasonable price.
For those who wish to have full-color images, a quality full-color
issue can be purchased for 25.00$. Content may vary in appearance
due to publisher policies.